KU-792-482

Ending Poverty

WITHDRAWN

Ending Poverty

Robin Marris

Thames & Hudson

To Clare Short, British Minister for International Development, whose White Paper, *Eliminating World Poverty*, published in 1997, provided much inspiration for this book

Many people and organizations have given valuable help and advice in the preparation of this book, but I should like to single out the Secretary of State and officials at the British Department of International Development; officials and experts at the United Nations; and, also, for major detailed written comments, Jae Edmonds, Alaknanda Patel, Amartya Sen and Adrian Wood. Yorick Blumenfeld, the general editor of the series, who conceived the idea for the book, gave constant moral support and radical advice, and the editorial team at Thames & Hudson enormously improved the original manuscript.

British Library Cataloguing-in-Publication Data
A catalogue record for this book is available from the British Library

ISBN 0-500-28114-9

Printed and bound in Slovenia by Mladinska Knjiga

Contents

PROLOGUE

This book was mainly written in the first part of 1998. It set out a programme for eradicating absolute poverty throughout the world between the years 2000 and 2050. At that time the world economic crisis, which eventually exploded in October 1998, was a threat but not a certainty. If a long and severe world slump is not in fact averted, the anti-poverty programme could be delayed by as much as a decade: 2050 becomes 2060. If there are further subsequent crises, the delay would be correspondingly greater. The avoidance of chronic crisis is a necessary, but not a sufficient, condition for the end of poverty.

In the section on global finance, the late '90s crisis threat is discussed but not fully evaluated. Now, in November 1998, it is absolutely clear that the threat is indeed severe, but it is not at all clear whether actions being taken by the major governments and international organizations will succeed in preventing it from getting worse.

The discussion of the causes of the crisis remains, in the author's opinion, valid. Although the crisis had a number of separate elements (in Japan, in Russia, in Latin America and on Wall Street), they had a common link – the unhealthy way in which the global financial system had developed in the past quarter century. It is possible that the end result may be significant reforms. If so, this particular crisis could actually end up by helping progress towards our long-term aims.

Autumn 1998

THE POOR CAN GET RICHER

In the twenty-first century the human race will face a unique challenge. Poverty could be virtually abolished and the gap between rich and poor nations hugely reduced. The process has already started, but must be accelerated. There is no need for the poor to get poorer. In recent years the rich have become richer, but the poor have also become less poor. Contrary to widespread belief, in the past half century the global gap between rich and poor has not widened. Nor, however, has it narrowed. In the year 2000 there will be six billion humans, of whom one and a half billion will still be suffering absolute poverty. All those in this depressed quarter of the human race will lack sufficient income to purchase a basic minimum living standard, and the great majority will lack both safe water supplies and any education.

In addition there will remain great inequality among people who are not absolutely poor. The average citizen of the First World has a standard of living seven times greater than that of the average citizen of the Third World. As between the poorest fifth of the respective populations of the two worlds, the difference is even greater – nearer to ten times. As well as inequality between countries there is also major inequality within countries: typically, both in the First and Third Worlds, after allowing for tax, the poorest 20 per cent of the population has no more than 10 per cent of total purchasing power and usually less. The combined effect of inequality between countries and inequality within countries means that the richest fifth of the population of the First World is no less than *fifty times* richer than the poorest fifth of the Third World. This situation is no longer tolerable and no longer necessary.

By the year 2050 the number of people in absolute poverty (measured by the standards of the year 2000) must be reduced to zero, the gap between the average living standard in the two worlds must be halved and the gap between the poorest fifth of the population reduced by two thirds. By the end of the twenty-first century both gaps should be eliminated altogether. What is now the Third World should have the same average standard of living as what is now called the First World.

Since the standard of living of the First World will continue to grow, if only slowly, the rate of development of the Third World will have to be fast enough to do the required catching up. While, over the course of the century, average income per head in the First World will multiply by a factor of four or five, that of the Third World will have to grow at around $3^1/2$ per cent a year, and over the century multiply by a factor of thirty.

Since world population will continue to increase until the end of the century (at which point it is almost certain to stabilize) the world's total economic activity will be growing considerably faster than income per head and will, in fact, also need to multiply by a factor of thirty.

Despite the apparently daunting scale of the numbers, and despite deep concerns over the environment, these targets are feasible. Since World War II there has already been a substantial reduction in absolute poverty: worldwide malnutrition and infant mortality rates have been reduced, adult literacy raised, and the purchasing power of large numbers of very poor people significantly increased. These changes have affected not millions, but rather hundreds of millions of families.

Why then has poverty persisted? Our species is so clever, we could already easily produce all that is needed to wipe out poverty. Why don't we do it? The answer is that we do not follow the principle of, 'from each according to their ability; to each according to their need'. Instead we base our system on a principle which is effective rather than humane, i.e. the principle of, 'from each *and* to each according to their personal ability and circumstances'. Poor people are poor because for one reason or another, by no means their own 'fault', they are unable to produce enough in the way of marketable goods and services to purchase a better standard of living. That is the way of the market economy.

Under this tough principle, despite war, genocide and economic depression, our species has achieved amazing progress in the past two centuries. While our worldwide population increased fivefold, our worldwide production of all kinds of goods and services increased nearly *fiftyfold*. That means income per head made tenfold gains. In contrast, during the preceding three centuries world production and income per head had hardly increased at all.

In this book, production per head means the same thing as income per head. In economists' jargon the total production of a nation is called 'Gross Domestic Product' or GDP; when it is given as per head of population it is called 'GDP per capita'. All calculations of the history of population and GDP in the various nations and regions of the world are here based on the works of Angus Maddison, especially his *Monitoring the World Economy 1820–1992* (1995), and on *Penn World Tables* Internet website.

Given the system, it was virtually inevitable that the extraordinary development of income per head would be unevenly distributed. The problem of correcting the resulting inequality is as much political and social as technical and economic. There are also massive problems in the environment, the most serious of which is global warming. The environment problem and the poverty problem interact. For example, as the distinguished Cambridge economist Partha Dasgupta has convincingly shown (*The Environment and Development Issues*, 1997 and 'The Economics of Poverty in Poor Countries', 1998), the circumstances of poor farmers often push them into degrading their own environment, thereby increasing their own poverty. Nevertheless, the paradox of poverty alongside prosperity is now quite unnecessary. If we fail, the fault will be ours.

It is in fact a great credit to the human race that soon after the end of the Cold War, an increasing number of eyes, academic and political, national and international, are now turned towards the world poverty problem. Statistics are much better and public policy is trying to be better. The leading international organizations such as the UN and the

World Bank are pioneering both concepts and policies. The British 'New Labour' government has distinguished itself by producing the 1997 White Paper, *Eliminating World Poverty: a Challenge for the 21st Century* – an outstandingly well-informed policy document that is at the same time both ambitious and realistic.

It is also to our credit that we have taken increasingly seriously the problem of the pressure of our own population on our own habitat. As a result, although our planet is going to become more crowded, it may not be impossibly so. In turn that makes the poverty problem the more tractable.

There are many people who feel much more pessimistic. It is widely believed that economic growth on the necessary scale to achieve the kinds of targets set out above would effectively destroy the planet's environment. These views are often held strongly by people who also have strong humanitarian instincts. Their fears are not unfounded, but can be exaggerated. As will be fully argued in Chapter 8 of this book, the problem of the environment is, with the aid of due effort, manageable. For those who want to help the poor, excessive pessimism can be counter-productive.

CHAPTER 1

THE HUMAN RACE'S GREAT ASCENT

The Expansion of Europe

In its first stages, the great economic explosion that began two centuries ago was uniquely a performance of north-western Europe and her English-speaking extensions in North America and Australasia – the countries which later became known, by implication, as the 'First World'. At the end of the eighteenth century, income per head in these countries was already twice as high as in the rest of the world. Two centuries later the difference had doubled. By that time, the richest countries of the First World had become more than ten times better off than the poorest of the countries of the 'Third World'.

Over the whole range of the nineteenth and twentieth centuries the population of the First World increased by a factor of no less than seven and much the same happened in the rest of the world. As a result the balance between the two populations in the year 2000 will be much the same as in the year 1800. Today, as then, only a tenth of the global population has the good fortune to live in the First World. The fundamental difference between the two eras is that in 1800 the First World had only about a fifth of world GDP, but two centuries later, with the same share of world population, the figure will be over a half.

The countries which later became Communist can be called the 'Second World'. The familiar term 'Third World' refers to all the rest. Because they had fallen behind, the Third World countries were also called the 'under-developed' countries; as they began to develop, this was changed to 'developing' countries.

A strong case can be made that in Britain, where the story began, the condition of the general masses did not at first improve at all. Well into the twentieth century a large slice of the British working class experienced chronic poverty. The story was similar in the rest of western Europe: middle and upper-class prosperity looking down on working-class penury. In the USA, although the white working class fared much better than in Europe, other groups had very mixed experiences, the worst of which, of course, fell on the people of African descent whose ancestors had been captured and brought over as slaves.

Then, through the paradoxical medium of World War II, the whole First World experienced a dramatic social transformation. From the day the war ended (indeed, in the civilian economies of the belligerent countries, before it ended) an economic condition of full employment gave almost every section of the working class large absolute gains, while almost every section of the middle class suffered relative losses. But average income per head was doing so well that all classes, except at the very top, made some gains. The improvement was generally sustained for the next quarter century – a Golden Age of full employment and brisk economic growth whose benefits were either evenly shared between classes or went slightly disproportionately to the less well-off. New countries – Japan, and some from southern Europe – joined the First World. The *United Nations Human Development Report* of 1997 aptly described the period as 'The Second Great Ascent' from human poverty. The changes were so great that the whole concept of a 'working class' had to be modified. The boundaries of the Third World also became fuzzier.

Finally in the last quarter of the century, in the English-speaking First World countries, there was another dramatic change of direction. While the top economic groups had a bonanza, the bottom groups at best stood still. As a result, many people have argued, a new 'underclass' emerged. At the millennium, as many as ninety million First World residents will be living at or below the absolute standard of the official poverty line in the United States. In the countries of continental western Europe, whose economies had grown particularly fast in the Golden Age, there was in the later period no obvious increase in economic inequality, but there was a big slow down in economic growth and a steady increase in unemployment.

West European unemployment, especially high among young workers and especially young women, caused 'social exclusion' but not so much poverty. Why? Because those countries had strong welfare systems. In effect, work was rationed. The young have to wait to take the places of the middle-aged and in the meantime subsist on welfare payments or in the 'grey' labour market.

The Rest of the World

What happened after 1950 to the other four-fifths of the world? Its population exploded and by the year 2000 will be close to five billion. Nevertheless, contrary to wide belief, not only did these countries' total production increase, but it did so by more proportionally than the growth in population. Income per head, therefore, grew significantly. But that single fact represents a major over-simplification. To see why, and thereby gain essential background for the whole story of human development since 1950, it is necessary to look at the special stories of three particular countries: Russia, China and Japan.

Although Tsarist Russia had begun some industrialization, in the last years before the 1917 Revolution she was still a very backward country. Her income per head was only one-third of the then average figure in the First World, and a large proportion of her agricultural population of serfs was certainly very poor indeed. After the Revolution, up to World War II, the Communist regime brought the income-per-head differential against the First World down to a half. Thereafter, until the fall of Communism in the late 1980s, no further relative gains were made, and in fact there was some slipping back. Since then the post-Communist disruption has turned slipping into grave decline. But under Communism, although the average standard of living was low, and despite the comfortable life-style of the political elite, total income was rather evenly distributed and, outside the Gulag labour camps, absolute poverty among ethnic Russians was virtually eliminated. Since the fall of Communism, unfortunately, that has not been the case.

On the criterion of income per head, Japan, at the turn of the nineteenth and twentieth centuries, was even further down the scale than Russia. But David Landes in *The Wealth and Poverty of Nations* (1998) has suggested that, as compared to the situation in Russia and many other countries, although the life of the Japanese peasant was hard, poverty was rare. Education was already superior.

Japan defeated Russia in a series of wars around 1905 and gave the Western Allies an extremely hard time in World War II. Nevertheless, when she attacked the US fleet at Pearl Harbor in December 1941, her income per head was only a third of her enemy's. Since her population was also smaller, her total production was only one-fifth of that of the USA, a fact which goes a long way to explain her eventual defeat. Despite being the first and, so far, the last country to be hit by atom bombs, Japan's subsequent economic performance was indeed miraculous. She did much more than catch up and join the First World: at one point she seemed set to overtake it. From 1992 onwards, however, a natural-slowing down in production growth was accompanied by a financial crisis, exacerbated by failures of the banking system and government mismanagement, which brought the country's economy to a halt. But what has been achieved has been achieved, and long-term absolute decline is unlikely.

Russia and Japan have between them 10 per cent of the world's population. China has 20 per cent. Under Communism, one way and another (including not only legal and moral restraint, but also government-caused famine), and despite the primitiveness of much of her rural society, China's population growth has been brought down to about $1^1/_2$ per cent a year – higher than in the First World and Japan, but significantly lower than in the rest of the Third World.

What then happened to production and poverty under Communism in China? Around 1950, not long after the old government had been overthrown, economic progress looked up. Then came the results of the megalomania of the later years of Mao Tse-tung. First the Great Leap Backward (when a large part of total labour time was spent melting down cooking pots to make steel); then the attempted socialization of agriculture which produced famines that killed maybe 3 per cent of the whole population; then some reversal of the agricultural policies and some improvement in production; then the Great Cultural Revolution, which appeared to destroy (but didn't) most of higher and much of secondary education; then the death of Mao; and then cautious economic reform, without democracy.

The dramatic result is shown in Charts 1, 2 and 3. In the first chart we see that over the long haul, while China's total population doubled, her poverty population was actually reduced. (In both Charts 1 and 2 the poverty line is defined as an income of less than one US dollar of standard purchasing power a day. The significance of the fact that no one could possibly survive in the USA on an annual income of $365 will be discussed in the next chapter.)

By contrast, in South Asia in the second half of the twentieth century, not only did the total population grow considerably faster than in China and Japan, the poverty population also increased – in fact, it nearly doubled. At the end of the twentieth century, although South Asia will have less than a quarter of the world's total population, the region will have nearly half of the world's poor.

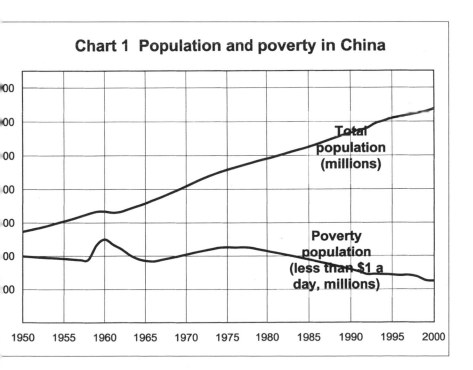

Chart 1 Population and poverty in China

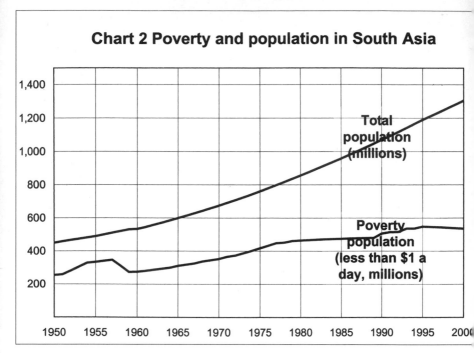

Chart 2 Poverty and population in South Asia

Total population (millions)

Poverty population (less than $1 a day, millions)

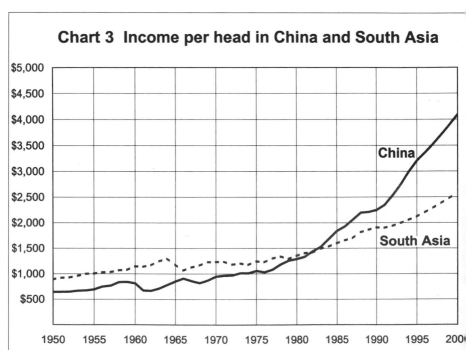

Chart 3 Income per head in China and South Asia

China

South Asia

Chart 3 shows the reason for this. The big success in Chinese poverty reduction began when the Great Leap Backward was reversed and economic growth took off. The fundamental reason why South Asia has fallen behind is that it has not taken off into fast economic growth.

More recently, in China and in East Asia generally the growth of living standards has become significantly more uneven. Some individuals and families have shot ahead economically. A large proportion of personal gains have been invested in the general economic growth, which until the mid-1990s, continued to be spectacular. But the families who trailed behind did not suffer absolutely, they continued to make small gains and absolute poverty continued to fall. Nevertheless, not without good reason the Chinese government has become genuinely concerned that rapid industrialization may be reproducing what happened in Britain in the nineteenth century when urban poverty replaced rural poverty.

In the remainder of the Third World (Latin America, North Africa, the Middle East and sub-Saharan Africa – over a billion people, a quarter of world population) there were also diverse experiences. The worst story unfolded among the twenty countries that lie between the Sahara desert and the river Zambezi and who will hold more people than China by the middle of the twenty-first century. They started from the lowest level and have not been helped by wars, misgovernment and droughts. Nevertheless, during the last quarter of the twentieth century, their income per capita did grow somewhat. The proportion of people below the $1-a-day poverty line (as high, but not higher, than in South Asia) remained constant. At the end of the century there are signs of recovery. Uganda, for twenty years desolated by tribal conflict and political horror, has recently, like the Republic of Ireland, experienced the beginning of a mini economic miracle. Latin America made modest but fairly continuous progress until the 1980s, then experienced a severe setback. As a result of a general financial crisis concerned with debt repayment, the GDP of some countries, rather than growing, actually declined, and at the end of the decade the GDP of the whole region was only a little higher than at the beginning. Since population continued to grow, average Latin

American income per capita declined absolutely. This 'lost decade' was in effect a development disaster.

Taking a longer view, most qualified critics would judge that Latin America's performance should have been much better. Brazil, for example, is a comparatively prosperous country. Yet as compared with South Asia, although average income per head is three times higher, her absolute-poverty performance is only moderately better. She has a total population of over 150 million, no less than 50 million of whom are below the $1-a-day line. It is significant that her biggest problem is in the north-east, which lies close in latitude to sub-Saharan Africa.

The Global Picture

Chart 4 gives an overview of global inequality and poverty since the mid-1960s. Countries are put in ascending order of income per head, and income per head is multiplied by the country's total population to give its total income. Then, for the poorest country we calculate the percentage it holds of world population (x-axis) and the percentage it holds of world income (y-axis). Thus we are plotting the share of income held by the poorest 5 per cent, then the poorest 10 per cent, then 15 per cent, and so on.

Top-end groups hold small shares of population and large shares of income. When we have cumulated to 100 per cent we have all the population and all the income. Therefore the curve bends back on itself. It starts at the bottom left and must end at the top right.

If all countries had the same income per head, the 'curve' would be a straight line between the two origins. This is the total-equality line: the further the curve deviates from it to the right, the greater the general extent of actual inequality. Because of the different growth rates of income per head for the different regions and countries of the world between 1965 and 1992, for every poor country that did badly, another did well; and for every mid-range country that did well, another did badly, and so on. The chart shows conclusively that it is simply not the case that the rich have been getting richer and the poor poorer. There has been neither a closing nor a widening of the gap.

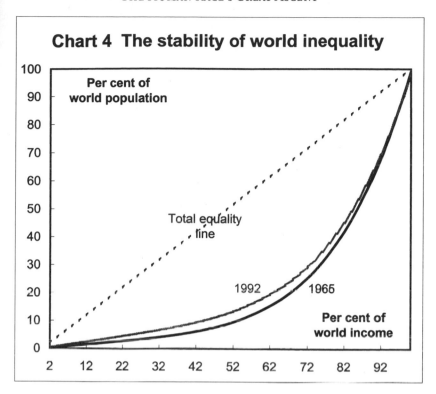

Chart 4 The stability of world inequality

Both rich and poor have become richer; neither, any more nor any less, on average, than the other. Inequality has remained constant.

(The United Nations sometimes claims that over the years international inequality has increased. Unfortunately, for this conclusion, they use calculations that, unlike their calculations relating to the $1-a-day absolute-poverty line, do not take account of the international differences in the cost of living – a method which yields a false result.)

As will be discussed in the following chapter, inequality is not the same thing as poverty. Between 1965 and 1992, the average income per head of the whole world increased by two-thirds. The similarity of the two curves in the chart means that the bottom 20 per cent of the world population also experienced a two-thirds gain. Since their starting point was extreme poverty, it was no big deal. But it was not nothing at all. Inevitably, a large number of people moved from below to above the $1 line. Precisely how many is not certain, but the recent

British Government White Paper (*Eliminating World Poverty*, 1997) suggests that, over half a century, half a billion people came out of absolute poverty. In other words, global poverty probably came down by a third. By the standards of the past, that was an achievement. By today's standards, it was far too little.

CHAPTER 2

THE MEANING OF POVERTY

The Problem of Measurement

If you ask people who are not themselves poor what they mean by poverty, most will give similar answers. They will describe a person or family surviving under conditions they themselves would find intolerable – undernourished, unhealthy, ill-clothed, badly housed and badly defended against misfortune. For example British research has shown that prosperous people see anyone trying to live only on the standard rate of unemployment benefit as really poor.

But for hundreds of millions of people in the Third World, the standard of living represented by the British unemployment benefit rate would seem like great prosperity. The same problem applies to comparisons made through history. One of the classic studies of poverty in the aftermath of the Industrial Revolution was made by Benjamin Seebohm Rowntree (of the great British Quaker chocolate dynasty) around the turn of the nineteenth and twentieth centuries. The research methods were rigorous. Lists were drawn up of the quantities of food, fuel and clothing and minor physical items (such as candles) of different types required for late-nineteenth-century bare minimum standards. The rental cost of minimum housing (outside toilet, no bath, no electric light) was added. All these items were carefully priced and then converted into budgets that would keep families of varying sizes just above the poverty line. Then a survey was made of working-class families in the city of York to find out how many had enough money for the basic budget. The finding was that during the phase when a working-class family had more than two children too young to be sent out to work, the majority of families were in poverty, that is, by the standards of the time, 'really poor'.

This research was repeated, using almost the same list of items, in the late 1930s. The figure for the proportion of working-class families who suffered absolute poverty during the vulnerable phase had come down to one in three.

When the survey was repeated soon after World War II, using, again, an only slightly modified list of essentials, it was impossible to find *any* people who, by the old standards, were now in poverty. As a result of the full employment created during the war and then sustained for a quarter century, by pre-war standards poverty had been totally eliminated. Of course, by the standards that developed after the war, poverty still existed.

Could one say in 1960 that a family whose home contained no bath, no radio and no inside toilet, and was lit only by candles, were not in poverty? And when we reach 1970, there is the question of the TV set; in 1980, the phone; in 1990, the car.

Measurement in the International Context

The United Nations, in its annual *Human Development Report,* classifies a Third World person as poor if, after adjusting for international differences in price levels, they are trying to live on less than $1 a day or $365 a year. But the UN does not believe that a person living in the First World could survive on such an income. Instead, for First World countries, they adopt the US Federal Government definition of poverty, which, for one person, at the price level of the year 2000, will be about $5500 a year, or almost *fifteen times* the Third World figure. For the Second World, the UN adopts a compromise figure, which, again adjusted to the year 2000, is about $1650 a year.

In Britain, the UN First World standard for four persons (that is, a purchasing power of about £250 a week) is not far from the total welfare payments (including rent allowance) to an unemployed family of four, one of whom is a young child. After food, rent and other obvious necessities, there would be maybe £30 over – no car, but a TV; an inside toilet; running hot water and hygienic fresh water. Maybe central heating is included in the rent. If this £30 is not carefully spent, the family will be undernourished.

Families on the $1-poverty line in the Third World will have few of these things. Two in five will not even have access to safe water.

There is clearly a fundamental problem in any comparison of poverty between the Third World and the First World, or over historical periods when average standards have risen significantly.

The United Nations, and other people and other organizations, do find it meaningful, in an important sense, to put the First and Third Worlds into the same frame of reference. We do believe that we are comparing like with like in such comparisons. We are not comparing the same 'real' income; we are comparing misery. We are saying that a family below the $1-a-day poverty line in the Third World is suffering a degree of economic deprivation that is comparable in misery to that of the social exclusion that results from the economic deprivation of a four-person family attempting to live on $20,000 a year in the United States – in the South Bronx district of New York, say, or in rural West Virginia where a family with no car would have difficulty with food supply comparable, in principle if not in severity, with the situation of a famine-struck family in the Third World. In fact, a poor white rural American family may own three cars, all old, and probably one that does not work. In the USA, a rise in the price of motor fuel hits the poor much harder than the rich. In Europe that state of affairs may not be far behind.

In short, the daily quantity of goods needed to provide a minimum quality of life is much greater in the First World than in the Third World. Similarly, the quantity of goods required to provide an acceptable minimum quality of life in the First World in the year 2000 is greater than it was in the year 1950, and greater still than in the year 1900.

The conclusion stretches beyond international comparisons. It also involves comparisons made within one country, at one time, between people. In some respects elderly retired people have less demanding needs than younger people; in other respects, such as medical needs, they have more. Physically disabled people clearly achieve a lower quality of life from a given income than those without disabilities. The rules and methods of the welfare states of all First World countries deliberately, and in various ways, take account of these things.

Poverty and 'Capability'

Amartya Sen, 1998 Nobel Prize Winner for Economics, has suggested a useful concept for describing the problem. In his book *On Economic Inequality* (1997), he argues that, rather than comparing money or detailed quantities of consumer goods, we should compare what he called 'capabilities'. Loosely, it is a similar term to 'quality of life'. More precisely, a person's capability is to be measured by the extent to which, for one reason or another, they are or are not able to do the various things they value doing, leading the kind of life they value living or being the kind of person they desire to be. These valued things, he suggested, may vary from the elementary, such as being adequately nourished, to the personal states, such as being able to take part in the life of the community.

This idea led Sen to a deeper definition of the concept of poverty itself, namely capability deprivation. A person is in poverty if they are unable to do many of the things they value doing. Obviously, the concept has two aspects. One aspect is the physical, social and psychological process that generates the menu of desires or aspirations; the other is the personal and social environment that constrains achievement. In a subsistence society, the main need is food and the main constraint is land. In a modern economy, needs, desires and aspirations are broader and the main constraint is money. But there are other important constraints in both cases. A subsistence-farming family may be deprived in comparison with another family occupying similar land because a leading member is disabled, or because of a different family structure. A modern-economy family with apparently sufficient money may also be deprived by reason of personal disability or by factors in the environment, such as poor infrastructure or air pollution.

The concept provides a convenient way of describing the relation between the UN's poverty lines for the First and Third Worlds. The UN is saying that to achieve a given level of capability, a First World family needs nearly fifteen times the daily quantity of goods and services than the quantity required to achieve the same level of capability as a Third World family.

The UN defines people subsisting below the respective dollar lines as suffering 'income poverty' (for example, below $15 in the UK, $5 in the Ukraine and $1 in India). An alternative term is 'absolute' poverty. It is an indirect measure only. We simply infer that a person with less than the required amount of money will be deprived. We cannot be certain that our inference is correct.

The United Nations Human Poverty Index

It is a problem, however, that capability is not inherently measurable. Although poverty researchers (Rowntree, for example) have long been used to measuring the extent to which a family is capable of being adequately nourished, until recently they were not accustomed to quantifying the broader elements suggested by Sen.

The UN, however, has made an interesting attack on the problem. In the *Human Development Report* it has published a numerical indicator based on a combination of five specific statistical indicators of physical deprivation, namely:

Percentage of total population expected to die under 40
Percentage of children under five judged to be malnourished
Percentage of illiterate adults
Percentage of people without access to safe water
Percentage of people without access to health services

The numerical indicator for an individual country – called by the UN the Human Poverty Index, or HPI – is an average of the five percentages. The UN uses the term 'human poverty' (as measured by the index) to contrast with income poverty. They are not the same thing. They result from different statistical procedures, although obviously they will be connected. A country or region with low average income per head will to some extent inevitably experience income poverty, but with good government, as for example in the Indian state of Kerala, it is possible, although not easy, for people living near $1 a day to have adequately nourished children, low illiteracy and safe water.

If we average Third World countries together, taking account of their different population sizes, we can infer from the UN report that about a third of all Third World young children are malnourished, 13 per cent of people will die before the age of forty, 20 per cent of adults have no education, 25 per cent of the population have no safe water and 20 per cent do not have any access to health services. If numbers are all kept in percentages, the average of the averages is close to 25 per cent. Thus one can conclude that roughly a quarter of the whole population of the Third World suffers human poverty.

The variation of the UN HPI around the average is enormous. The figure for countries such as Cuba, Chile, Singapore and Costa Rica is around 5, in sub-Saharan Africa around 60; in South Asia it is around 40 and in China just under 20. There is also great variation between the different regions of large countries. In the Indian state of Kerala the figure is as low as 15 compared to the Indian average of 40. Compared to the national average of 20, in the western provinces of China it is 45, while Beijing is as low as 10. The figure for north-east Brazil is comparable to South Asia and three times the figure for south-east Brazil.

The UN has calculated the HPI in the same way for all Third World countries. The very nature of the concept of capability, however, implies that valid indicators will vary between societies in accordance with the economic, cultural and physical environment. An index that is suitable for the Third World is therefore unlikely to be suitable for the First World. In the First World, malnutrition among children in the 'underclass' is quite prevalent, but the class is not a large proportion of the total population. Consequently the proportion of all young children who are malnourished is small. Ninety-nine per cent of people have a primary education, so few are illiterate. More than 95 per cent live past the age of forty. The water supply is generally safe. Public health services – or, in the US, Medicare and Medicaid – are in theory available to all. The UN, therefore, gives a table containing an alternative indicator list for the First World, namely:

> Percentage of total population expected to die under age 40
> Percentage of working population who are unemployed
> Percentage of secondary-school-age young people who are not enrolled in secondary school.

Notice that the first item is the same as the first item in the Third World list, but the others are appropriately different. In the First World, the typical person has secondary education and has a job, and to be without these things is to be deprived. The UN does not, however, attempt to calculate a general index from this table because the numbers are too small. If they did, Japan, Sweden and Norway would have stood out well in 1994; the UK and Germany not well; and the USA and France would be somewhere in the middle. By 1998, with lower unemployment in the UK and higher unemployment in Japan, the relationships might have changed.

The general result, as estimated by the author for the year 2000, is shown in the table below. The second and third columns represent two of the components of the UN HPI. There is a connection, but not a hard and fast one, between the columns. Education and sanitation cost money. The charge that is currently levied, directly or indirectly, on the average First World low-income household to pay for water supplies and sewage disposal (the key to safe water) can be anything

WORLD POVERTY IN THE YEAR 2000				
Income Poverty Third World: Second World: First World:	**means less than** $1 a day $5 a day $15 a day	People in income poverty % of total pop.	People with no safe water % of adult pop.	People with no education % of total pop.
China		27	38	19
Rest of East Asia		13	28	14
South Asia		44	16	31
Western Islam (North Africa, Turkey, Syria, Lebanon, Saudi Arabia, Afghanistan, Iraq, Iran)		5	13	16
Sub-Saharan Africa		35	39	21
Latin America		19	20	8
Total above ('Third World')		28	26	20
Ex-Communist ('Second World')		20	not known	negligible
Rest of World ('First World')		10	negligible	negligible
Whole World		25	21	16

For a discussion of the problems of international comparisons of poverty levels, please see pages 22–30.

up to 50 US cents per head per day. That would be an impossible slice of $1 a day, but is a reasonable slice of $15 a day. Nevertheless, China, which has a good record in education and income-poverty reduction, faces major problems over her water supply.

The table shows that at the outset of the twenty-first century one in four (25 per cent) of the whole world population, or one and a quarter billion souls, will be suffering income poverty. In the First World, on the $15-a-day standard, the figure will be one in ten. In South Asia, on the $1-a-day standard, it will be not far short of an incredible one in two. Safe-water deprivation is much less severe in South Asia than in Africa, in China or East Asia. In China and East Asia many people who are not in income poverty will still lack safe water.

In the First and Second Worlds, there is much variation in the extent of secondary and higher education, but virtually no one escapes primary education. By contrast, in the Third World, averaged over both sexes (as in the table) no less than one person in five (and among women the figure is worse) will have no primary education and thus be unable to read or write. That figure is worst in South Asia, where it reaches up to one in three, and least bad in East Asia and Latin America.

That is the summary of the general scale of human poverty which challenges us in the twenty-first century. On the global averages, though severe, it looks manageable. In major regions such as South Asia and Africa, it looks daunting. But the more daunting it looks, the greater should be the effort devoted to facing and defeating it.

Poverty and Inequality

Why? What would be wrong if things went on as they have been? Chart 4 (p. 19) showed that this would mean that the average real income of the Third World continued to grow at only a slow or moderate rate about equal to the growth rate of the First World. Income or absolute poverty in the Third World would continue to decline at a moderate pace, but the proportionate gap between the living standards of the two worlds would remain unchanged. In addition, taking one country with another, the average amount of inequality within nations (as shown by the Deininger and Squire data set maintained on the World Bank Internet site) would also remain constant, as it has done, in fact, for the past quarter of a century. With inequality constant both within and between countries, the whole world-wide distribution of income among families and individuals would thus be constant. For every individual who went up in the economic scale, there would be another, somewhere in the world who went down.

There are people who would say that, provided the average living standard was growing, that scenario would be quite acceptable. There are many others who would say that since the existing level of inequality is much too high, it would be intolerable. Here is a head-on conflict between the 'absolute' and 'relative' concepts of deprivation. As the following quotation from the London *Times* shows (13 December 1997), it has major political overtones.

> Claims that the number of people suffering hardship increased under the Tories [British Conservative administration, 1979–97] are to be dismissed by a right-wing think-tank. They say that among households in the worst-off 10 per cent of the population, there have been large increases in central heating and in ownership of fridge-freezers, cars and videos. The director of the Rowntree Foundation rejected the report saying, 'Nobody disputes that the rich got 60 per cent better off and the poor gained little or nothing.'

The United Nations states that British poverty increased sharply during the 'Thatcher' period (*Human Development Report 1997*). Although they do not say so, they must be referring to relative poverty. Yet elsewhere in their great report, when they speak of poverty without qualification they usually mean absolute poverty.

The same problem is present in all inter-country comparisons. According to the UN, 30 per cent of all the people of the Republic of Ireland are suffering from income poverty. By contrast the figure for Mexico is given as 10 per cent and the figure for Poland as 13 per cent. But it is quite apparent that the poorest segment of the people of Ireland are better off than their counterparts in Poland and, of course, very much better off than their counterparts in Mexico, but Ireland, for better or for worse (and partly no doubt because of her geographical location) is classified as First World. Currently experiencing fast economic growth, she is still a much poorer country, overall, than the USA. But as a First World country she is assigned the $15-a-day North American-based poverty line. If, with the same economic features, she was assigned the eastern European poverty line, her 'absolute' poverty index would be more than halved.

Why not assign Ireland and other countries variable poverty lines based not on geographical location but on average per capita income? The answer is that in doing so we would move straight away from the absolute to the relative concept of poverty. Should we or shouldn't we?

Inequality and Welfare

The question is, when assessing the economic performance of a society do we only look at what happened to the poor, or may we take some account of what happened to the rich?

Ever since the human race took up agriculture, both purchasing power and quality of life (capability) have been unequally shared out. Rightly or wrongly, sadly or happily, extreme egalitarian communities have not survived. Not only are some people poor and some people rich, but some rich are richer than other rich and there is also a whole spectrum of prosperity among middle classes. Thus inequality affects all classes, not just the poor, and as a result, for example, of a shift between the middle and the upper classes it would be possible for the general inequality to change while the situation of the lowest classes remained constant.

Nevertheless, in a very important way the two problems (poverty and inequality) are closely connected. They are connected by a common relationship to the general welfare of society. Economists call this Social Welfare. It is defined as an aggregate, or 'function' in the mathematical sense, of the economic well-being (economic happiness) or 'welfare' of all the individuals of which a society is composed. Because an extra dollar obviously means more to a poor person than a rich one, Social Welfare does not depend on average income alone; it also depends on distribution. If two societies have the same average income but different distribution, it is mathematically certain that the one with less inequality has greater Social Welfare, that is, greater average economic happiness.

Equality versus Productivity

Why not organize society so that in one way or another, inequality does not develop? The answer lies in the reason why egalitarian societies have not survived. The entire edifice of human economic productivity is based on the ability both to encourage and to maximize the benefits of technological progress by the process of market exchange. This means that not only goods but also labour services are exchanged for a market price. It also means that inherited property has a market price giving economic power to the beneficiary. People are born with different endowments of ability, property and opportunity for personal advancement by means of education, effort and social contacts, and so have different market prices. The market system inevitably creates inequality. Worse, the market system depends on the incentives created by inequality for its economic efficiency. The incentive to work is the lure of income. The fundamental cause of the Chinese famines of the early 1960s was that, in creating the socialist agricultural communes, the government separated the work of the peasants from their rewards. The government took the crops and rewarded all workers equally with fixed rations of consumer goods such as food and housing. Many peasants gave up bothering to work, and the result was, tragically, peasant starvation.

Recently China has developed a system of town and village enterprises, mainly involved in labour-intensive manufacturing. These entities are to some extent worker-owned, and undoubtedly generate less inequality than typical First World manufacturing businesses. Neverthless, the Chinese town and village enterprises contain very definite economic incentives. In particular, they employ numerous workers who are not members and are paid only market wages. Thus they sustain a degree of economic inequality. Significantly, the town and village enterprises have been very successful. Some employ as many as ten thousand souls, and in total they employ over a million people. They have also made a considerable contribution to China's exports.

In the First World, all governments by means of tax patterns and the Welfare State 'interfere' to some degree with income distribution in an egalitarian direction. The Thatcher–Reagan era represented a deliberate but only partial reversal of the redistributive policy that had evolved from the beginning of the century.

Why did the British and American electorate's support, or at least permit, the Thatcher–Reagan policies for so long? Was it because the typical voter believed that she or he would be better off? Or was it because they were persuaded that these policies would on balance benefit the whole community, i.e. increase Social Welfare? On the latter view, even after allowing for the fact that an extra dollar is worth more to the poor than to the rich, the gains to those who gained from the Thatcher–Reagan policies would outweigh the losses of the losers. The gain in average income per head attributable to supposedly improved incentives would outweigh the losses due to the change in distribution.

Can Social Welfare be Measured?

The concept of Social Welfare is thus a powerful mental tool for thinking about the problems of poverty and inequality, but it suffers from a rather crucial handicap. We can measure people's incomes and maybe their capabilities, but we cannot measure their welfare. We can be sure that the value of money diminishes with income but we have no simple way of quantifying this effect. During the twentieth century, the profession of economics was, in fact, overtaken by grave philosophical doubts as to whether, as a matter of principle, 'utility' or welfare could be measured at all. It was particularly in doubt whether utility could be measured as a quantity that could be compared between individuals and it was said that any such attempted comparisons must be intrinsically 'unscientific'. These assertions were not, however, based on medical or biological evidence. In truth, there is indeed a difficult scientific problem in making economic comparisons between individuals, namely that the relation between 'economic satisfaction' and happiness is at present elusive. A person suffering from clinical depression may continue to feel desperately unhappy even after the news of a large financial windfall. Worse, an unhappy mood may be cured by a course of Prozac rather than good news on the economic front.

No one, however, is suggesting that the task of eliminating world poverty should be evaded by distributing Prozac to millions of starving people. Improved psychological mood, however desirable per se, is obviously no substitute for improved long-term capability. In consequence the proposition that 'inter-personal' utility comparisons are impermissible is now largely discredited. The proof of the pudding is in the eating. Economists are deeply concerned about poverty and also general inequality. Without inter-personal comparisons their concern would be meaningless. Poverty could not be measured. We would not know who the poor were.

Consequently, contemporary economists discuss practical problems as if the economic welfare of different individuals were commensurable, even though, in the present state of science, precise measurements cannot actually be made. For example, the fact that in the past quarter century world average income increased while inequality remained constant makes it mathematically certain that world Social Welfare increased.

Utilitarianism versus Egalitarianism

Is Social Welfare to be regarded as the simple arithmetic sum of individual welfare? Many people would think the answer must be, 'Yes', others are not so sure. The first group are described as Utilitarians, the second as Egalitarians. The issue between them is basically philosophical. Imagine two societies, one with high productivity and high inequality, the other with the opposite characteristics. Suppose the countervailing effects of productivity and inequality just cancelled out so that both had the same average economic happiness. The Utilitarian would say that the two countries thus had the same level of Social Welfare and no further judgment could be made between them. The Egalitarians would say, on the contrary, there is a moral value to equality (or better a moral disapproval of inequality) which should also be taken into account in evaluating Social Welfare. They would say that the less unequal of the two societies was 'better', and had higher Social Welfare.

One way to pursue the debate is to imagine a group of people discussing which of the two societies would be preferable, assuming that in either case these people could expect average economic happiness. Given that average economic happiness in the two societies is expected to be the same, would these imaginary individuals be indifferent, or would they, nevertheless prefer the more egalitarian society on the ground that they would be morally pleased that it contained fewer poor people?

Although the question sounds abstract, and may never be overwhelmingly resolved, it is very illuminating. It helps concerned people better to understand their own thinking. The author of this book is an Egalitarian. That is why the Action Programme for the twenty-first century calls for not only the global elimination of absolute poverty but in addition a massive reduction of general inequality.

CHAPTER 3

THE FUTURE OF THE WORLD POPULATION

Population growth is a crucial factor in any assessment of poverty prospects. This can be seen by a simple calculation. The British Government 1997 White Paper proposes the target of halving the proportion of the world's population living in absolute poverty by the year 2015. The world poverty table (p. 27) shows that in the year 2000 this will be 25 per cent. Twenty-five per cent of six billion is one and a half billion. If this is to be reduced to $12^1/2$ per cent in fifteen years, to what base should we apply the new percentage? What will world total population be by then?

The answer is that if the world population continued to grow at the same annual percentage rate, namely a little under 2 per cent a year, as it actually grew in the thirty years before 1990, by 2015 the six billion would be eight and a half billion. Twelve and a half per cent of eight and a half billion is roughly one billion. So compared to the year 2000, the absolute numbers in absolute poverty in 2015 would be down by half a billion, that is, by about one third. The number remaining in absolute poverty would still be as high as a billion.

But if the world population growth slowed down by a reasonable amount, the results could be very different. The reduction of the absolute numbers in absolute poverty could go up from a third to a half, and the numbers remaining in poverty could go down by hundreds of millions.

The Doctrines of Malthus

The problem is partly circular, because not only is it easier to reduce poverty if population growth slows down, but the chances of a slow-down are, in fact, higher the more rapidly poverty is reduced. The first person to see this was Thomas Malthus (1766–1837). Influenced

35

by the results of the new population census, which gave the first clear evidence that the human population was briskly increasing, he developed a very simple idea. The human race depends on food which depends, in turn, on land. Land supply is fixed or constrained. If the human population increases persistently, it will press on the supply of land and food. There will be war, pestilence and famine. The death rate will rise and the birth rate will fall. So the population growth will be stopped or slowed until the population level has been brought back into balance with the land and food supply. Prosperity will return. Unfortunately, prosperity will cause population growth to resume and the cycle of misery will then be repeated.

Most of the pain of this 'cyclical equilibrium' would fall on the poor. In the phase when the population is growing fast, more people will be seeking work and the purchasing power of the wages of the labouring class would be driven down towards the subsistence level. The general outlook was dismal.

Simplistic as it seems today, the idea was and remains very powerful. In the first hundred years following Malthus, it was completely discredited. Then in the mid-1960s it re-emerged in the form of neo-Malthusianism where the constraining factor was no longer literally the world supply of cultivable land but rather the total natural resources of the planet. The 'Green' movement, expressing general concern about population pressure on the total environment, is thus neo-Malthusian.

One of Malthus's proposals for reducing the burden of his dismal prediction was for a law requiring every priest conducting a marriage to preach a sermon against bringing children into the world who could not be adequately supported; in short, he proposed either contraception (which, in those days, although widely practised in one way or another, was not spoken of) or sexual abstinence.

There were two fundamental things actually happening around him throughout his lifetime that Malthus did not see. First, that the combined effects of technological change and social re-organization (including forcing peasants off the land to make way for large farms) could permit major increases in the general productivity of agriculture: sharp gains in output per acre and output per worker went hand in hand. Second, that the people taken out of agriculture would supply the labour for the Industrial Revolution, which in turn created the basic conditions for the Great Ascent of the human race, involving massive new supplies of both food and manufactured goods available to the population as whole. The grain of truth which remained (it was more like a stone than a grain) was that it took the best part of a hundred years for the working class to benefit and for urban poverty to begin to decline.

Malthus in the First World

In the meantime, the proof of the anti-Malthus pudding in the First World was in the history. As we have already seen, in the two hundred years following the publication of Malthus's essay, the population of the First World increased seven times, while poverty was eventually greatly reduced. The supply of food to the First World increased sufficiently to feed all the new mouths at least as well as before, while the share of agricultural activity in First World employment was drastically reduced. Some of the new food supply came from imports from First World colonies in the Third World, but a large part was simply due to the increased productivity of domestic agriculture. At the end of the twentieth century, the United States, with *less than 2 per cent* of her population in agriculture, produces more than enough food for her whole population and is also a vigorous food exporter. By contrast, there are still Third World countries with 80 per cent of their population in agriculture which often need to import food or have to experience famine.

Eventually, as we know, the rate of growth of First World population slowed. Currently it is running at less than a half of one per cent per annum – a weighted average of one per cent in the United States and about two-tenths of one per cent in the rest of the First World. Why did this slow-down occur? According to the Malthus theory, prosperity should have produced an increase in births and a decline in deaths. What actually happened was that first the death rate came down, then, after a delay, the birth rate, instead of rising, also fell. Why did the birth rate fall, and why the delay? The answer is that most married couples want to have a given number of children, say two to six, who will have a reasonable chance of surviving to adulthood. If they expect that some of their children will die in infancy they will tend to aim for more births. The higher the infant mortality rate the higher the birth rate. In one way or another, consciously or unconsciously, human populations responded by tacit adjustments of the average age of marriage, by primitive contraception, or by various taboos (such as, on sexual intercourse for a number of months after a birth) creating sexual abstinence.

The first effect of the Great Ascent in the First World took the form of health improvements which reduced the infant mortality rate. Naturally, however, people were slow to perceive the implications of the changed mortality prospects, and continued to give birth at the old rate. Thus while the death rate fell, the birth rate held up, and total population growth inevitably accelerated. Gradually people began to adjust and gradually the Total Fertility Rate (average total number of lifetime births per woman) came down. More than two hundred years after the onset of the Industrial Revolution, the population growth of the First World appears finally almost to have halted. In those intervening years, it grew from 100 million to 700 million.

There is a major controversy among economists, of great importance to the future in the Third World, as to whether rapid population growth did not in fact encourage the growth of industrial productivity. The argument (and it is a strong one) is that larger populations mean larger markets and hence more opportunities for taking advantage of the economic benefits of large-scale production. In short, the whole historical process is seen as circular. The Industrial Revolution caused the population explosion and the population explosion encouraged the Industrial Revolution. Notice, however, that the argument applies to industry and not to agriculture. There are some social scientists today who believe that the growth of agricultural populations in Third World countries also helps, rather than hinders, agricultural productivity, but others, probably a majority (and including the author) strongly disagree. The disagreement is important, because if the former school were correct, one could no longer say, as was said at the beginning of this chapter, that population growth was necessarily a hostile factor in the war on poverty.

Malthus in the Third World

What happened to population in the Third World after World War II was in some respects similar to what had previously happened in the First World. But a fundamental difference was that medical advance preceded the process of industrialization: cheap and simple measures quickly reduced both the general death rate and the infant mortality rate, while the bulk of the population still remained at a low productivity level in agriculture. In the first quarter century after World War II the overall death rate in Third World countries was precisely halved. The infant death rate came down by almost as much. These were very rapid changes. Inevitably births did not immediately adjust: in 1975 the Third World Total Fertility Rate was almost as high as in 1950. But eventually, precisely as the theory predicts, Third World women, obviously aided by birth-control campaigns, began to realize that they needed fewer births to create a reasonably sized surviving family, and the Total Fertility Rate at last began to decline. In fact, in the next quarter century, this crucial figure virtually halved. The great majority of people in the First World are unaware of this.

The problem is that, just as had previously happened in the First World, the Third World population, already nearly ten times as great as the First World population, continued to increase absolutely at a brisk rate. Having gained more than one and a half billions from 1950 to 1975, by the year 2000 it will have increased by further one and a half billions. Given that fertility was by now declining sharply, how could this happen?

Firstly there is an inevitable lag, already discussed, between a decline in the number of children that the typical family, consciously or unconsciously, intends to have. Secondly, the overall death rate (including adults), now affected not only by medical advance but by improved nutrition following the so-called Green Revolution in agriculture, also continued to fall fast. Population growth did not, therefore, slow down. In the late '80s, the annual percentage growth of Third World Population, at over 2 per cent, was exactly the same as it had been in the early '50s. This fact caused a great deal of alarm and despondency until recently, and also stimulated the world community to think ever more seriously about birth control. Public policy became increasingly positive, and religious opposition was increasingly isolated.

At last, in the final decade of the century, as the birth rate continued to decline steadily, while the decline in the death rate became less rapid, Third World population growth rate significantly slowed: in the five years before 1990, it had still been running at 2 per cent a year; in the following five years it fell to $1^3/_4$ per cent a year. Small as it may seem, such a sharp decline in so short a time is highly significant. It is backed up by the fact that in every age group in the total population of Third World women of child-bearing age, fertility statistics declined. That is a strong indicator that the downward trend of the population growth rate is unlikely to be reversed.

The Global Population

A fundamental aim of development policy is to reduce the differences between the First, Second and Third Worlds. We are looking for One World. This does not mean cultural uniformity but it does mean a great reduction in economic diversity. It is to be hoped that the mischance of being poor will no longer be heavily influenced by where one was born.

Maybe the project will take a century, maybe less. But on the time-scale of a century, the population 'problem' must also be seen as global rather than regional. The story that has just been unfolded about the Third World has a One World equivalent.

Chart 5 shows the dramatic picture of the worldwide downward race of birth rates and death rates since World War II. It is of course heavily influenced by the story of the Third World, which has more than 80 per cent of the total population. Thus we see the crucial moment in the 1980s, indicated by the long arrow, when the global 'population transition' arrived. By studying the underlying trends of

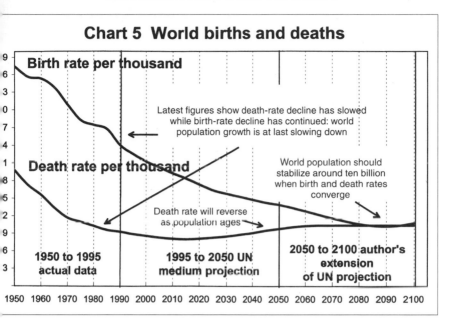

Chart 5 World births and deaths

Birth rate per thousand

Latest figures show death-rate decline has slowed while birth-rate decline has continued: world population growth is at last slowing down

Death rate per thousand

World population should stabilize around ten billion when birth and death rates converge

Death rate will reverse as population ages

1950 to 1995 actual data

1995 to 2050 UN medium projection

2050 to 2100 author's extension of UN projection

1950 1960 1970 1980 1990 2000 2010 2020 2030 2040 2050 2060 2070 2080 2090 2100

'age-specific' fertility rates and morbidity (death) rates, the United Nations Population Division has been able to make quite confident forecasts for the next half century, and the author has with reasonable confidence carried the UN curves forward to the end of the century. It is definitely reasonable to expect that the two curves will join before the year 2100. In fact, the UN has offered an alternative forecast, 'Low Variant', where the event occurs considerably sooner: it is based on the by no means improbable assumption that the fertility decline will accelerate. (There is also a 'High' forecast, implying a rather implausible slow-down in the decline in fertility, thus reversing the whole tendency of the past fifty years.) When the birth-rate and death-rate curves join up, the world population will have stabilized.

Three cheers! Well not entirely. See Chart 6 (p. 42), which, in place of birth and death rates, plots the actual population. The heavy line at the top is the Malthusian nightmare. It is, however, no more than a straight projection of the path that the world population seemed to be following up to the early 1980s. If that actually happened there would be fifty billion humans by the year 2100, that is, nearly ten times the present number, which would be insupportable. Following Malthus's

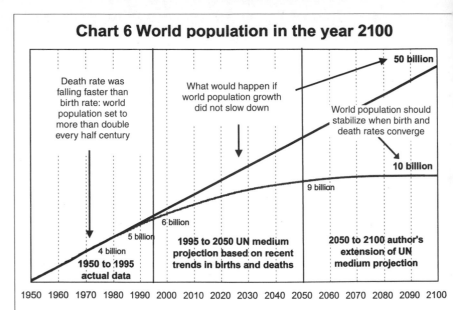

Chart 6 World population in the year 2100

argument, it could not happen. There would have been a great cull of humans, probably by nuclear war.

Fortunately, a different scenario is unfolding, as shown on the lower curve. But that the curve does not show a comfortable situation. Compared with six billion in the year 2000, by 2015 there will be seven billion humans, and by 2050, nine billion. After that, things look better – slow growth to stability around ten billions at the end of the twenty-first century. In short, our numbers are still going to double.

If there are more people in the world as a whole, there are more people in danger of being born into poverty, and the effort required to avert the danger has to be all the greater. The title of the 1997 British Government White Paper was *Eliminating World Poverty: a Challenge for the 21st Century*. Suppose one were to interpret those words as implying that after achieving the target of halving the *proportion* of people in absolute poverty by the year 2015, the next step would be to reduce the absolute number by the middle of the century to virtually zero. Between that year and 2050, Chart 6 shows, the total world population will go up to nine billion. During that time, on the one hand, some of poverty population will die, and, on the other hand, new surviving children will be born into it. So, in saying that we will eliminate world poverty by the middle of the century, we are saying, in effect, that we will make an effort equivalent to taking *two and a quarter* billion people out of poverty in half a century. This is a perfectly feasible task, but it is made heavier by population growth. If the world population grew more slowly, for example, if the figure followed the United Nations 'Low Variant', the task would be so much the lighter. Following this argument, population-control policy is an intrinsic part of anti-poverty policy. All praise and moral support should be given to governments that pursue vigorous and rigorous population-control policies. Opposition from religious and other irrational influences must be passionately resisted.

Chapter 4

Poverty and Economic Growth

> Economic growth is the prime means of creating income and
> employment opportunities. . . . Without growth. . . the poor will only be
> able to make insignificant improvements in their livelihoods. . . .'
>
> British Government White Paper, *Eliminating World Poverty*, 1997

In the year 2000 the total income of those defined by the United
Nations as the poor of the world will be just 4 per cent of the total
income of the whole world, a quarter of the world's people with less
than a twentieth of the world's income. Why not simply levy a tax of
five cents in the dollar on all the world's non-poor and hand it over
as a cash subsidy? The average income of the poor would be doubled
overnight, and most would be taken out of poverty. If the tax were
levied on First World citizens only, it would obviously have to be
higher, in fact about double.

Every reader will have an answer: it violates the principles of the
market economy; it would be bad for incentives; it would create global
'welfare dependency'; it would not directly increase either the employment or the productivity of the poor; it would be no more than a
temporary solution; and so on and so forth.

The simplest answer, however, is that whether it would be a good
idea or not, it is not going to happen. By means of the Welfare State, a
good deal of cash redistribution occurs within First World countries,
and the international aid programme has transferred modest
amounts of income, equivalent to a tax of less than one cent in the
dollar, from the First World to the Third World. But we do not yet have
world government, and international transfers on the scale required
are not in the realm of practical politics. Within the Third World itself,
the non-poor, who are actually two-thirds of the population, are on

average living at a level less than one-fifth of that of the non-poor in the First World. Although some Third World countries have a small class of people who are disturbingly rich by any standards, the great majority of the Third World's non-poor are not rich. This fact obviously adds to the difficulty (or impossibility) of trying to solve the world's poverty problems by simple cash transfers.

If simple cash redistribution is ruled out, there are in logic only two ways in which poverty can be reduced. Either the productivity and earnings of the poor must be raised relatively to those of the non-poor, or the productivity and earnings of the whole society must advance with all sections advancing together. Many people see the former as the most feasible and significant solution to the problem of the 'new poor' in the First World, but in the Third World it is more a doubtful prescription. Economic progress is a collective effort. In the Third World, entrepreneurship, organization and effort on the part of the non-poor are essential ingredients in any recipe for enhancing the productivity of the actual poor. Indeed, there is evidence, especially from East Asia, that a certain degree of inequality in the rate of income and welfare improvement is inevitable if the first stages of 'take-off' are to be reinforced and sustained. The reason is that although capital from abroad represents a highly significant contribution, the greater part of the savings and investments required to support fast, sustained economic growth must ultimately come from the home economy. Over a period of five years ending in 1997, the total amount of capital, public and private, flowing from the First World to the Third World spectacularly trebled (the main factor was private money going to East Asia). But, in fact, the total flow represented no more than $60 per year per head of Third World population, which is at most a fifth of the total investment annually required to support a reasonable total Third World growth rate.

Stephen Triantis, writing in 1995, observed that people whose incomes have recently increased rapidly especially in East Asia, are likely to save and invest large proportions of their gains. In the 1980s and 1990s in some East Asian countries, such as Malaysia and Singapore, private savings thus stimulated may have represented capital investment at very high figures of the order of $1000 per head per year. In Latin America, unfortunately, the same has not occurred. This may be partly because growth has been much less rapid (the problem is circular, because lack of investment is one reason for slow growth), and partly because of a culture among the economically fortunate tending to encourage consumption and the investment of savings abroad rather than in the domestic economy.

Two Meanings of Growth

Unfortunately, the expression 'economic growth' has two distinct meanings – related but different – which are not always recognized in public discussion. In both cases we are speaking of long-term growth, averaged over at least ten years rather than what is meant when financial journalists write, for example, that 'last year the economy grew by 2 per cent'. In one case we are speaking of the growth of total income and production, and in the other we are speaking of income per head of population. In the Third World the significance of the distinction is obvious. If total production grows (long-term) at 2 per cent and population also grows at 2 per cent, income per head is constant. Unless there is a major change in the share-out between classes, the proportion of the population in absolute poverty will also therefore be constant. Furthermore, the absolute numbers in absolute poverty will actually be *growing* at 2 per cent, that is, doubling in less than half a century. By contrast, if total income is growing at 4 per cent, with population still growing at only 2 per cent, average income per head is growing at 2 per cent. Inside less than half a century average income per head will double and, since even below the absolute-poverty line some people, unfortunately, are poorer than others, it is not unlikely that the proportion in absolute poverty will be more than halved.

If the share-out between classes really is constant, as income rises not only do the average percentage gains of the poor equal those of the non-poor but also the different sub-groups among the poor make equal percentage gains. In this case it is probably possible to halve the number of people below the poverty line by means of an overall increase in average income per head of between 50 and 75 per cent.

The British Government White Paper of 1997 desires to achieve this target by the year 2015, that is (if we take the year 2000 as a base), inside fifteen years. This means an average Third World growth rate of income per head over the whole period between 3 per cent and $3^1/2$ per cent. Since the Third World population will be growing at $1^1/2$ per cent, the growth rate of total Third World GDP will need to be maybe as high as 5 per cent. That is a higher figure, but not impossibly higher, than the corresponding figure implied for the whole span of time up to the 2050 in the targets set out in the Introduction to this book. The British Government is suggesting an early push. But their implied growth rate is quite comparable with the rate which the Third World experienced over the decade before the onset of the East Asian economic crisis in 1997, which, although essentially financial in origin, will probably cause a serious slowing-down of real growth. In the absence of further setbacks, therefore, the British target is at the limit of the intrinsically feasible.

In the First World, the relation between the significance of total growth and per capita growth is almost reversed. Whereas in the Third World the growth of income per head is essentially the result of the twin processes of agricultural rationalization and industrialization, the First World has long completed industrialization and is entering a phase of 'de-industrialization' involving not only a shift of the labour force into the service sectors but also a persistent decline in the average annual hours of paid employment undertaken by the working-age population. Output per worker-hour in industry and services continues to rise, while output per head of total population lags behind.

The resulting process is governed by a fundamental piece of arithmetic which states that the annual percentage growth of total output is equal to the annual percentage growth in output per worker-hour *plus* the annual percentage growth in total employment (total number of person-hours worked). So in a most important way the equation can be turned around to throw light on an outstanding problem of the First World at the end of the twentieth century, namely insufficient employment. The annual percentage growth of total employment is equal to the annual percentage growth of total output *minus* the percentage growth of output per worker-hour.

There are two vital implications. First, if for any reason the growth rate of total production is less than the growth rate of productivity, employment will not be growing at all, rather it will be declining. Second, anything which can be done to increase the rate of growth of *total* output, relative to the growth of productivity, is beneficial to employment.

As we shall discuss in Chapter 6, inadequate growth of employment is the prime cause of the 'new poverty' in the First and Third Worlds. The problem can be reduced if the growth of total production can be increased. In the First World, the way to poverty reduction is acceleration of growth in the sense of total production, that is, total GDP, rather than, as in the Third World, GDP per capita.

The Keys to Third World Growth

Up until the mid-1980s it seemed that the attention that thinkers and political leaders in both the First and Third World since the end of World War II had devoted to the problem of redressing the world's economic balance seemed to have been without result. The income per capita of the typical Third World country grew steadily but not rapidly. In fact, although the average growth rate was significantly higher than that experienced before 1950, it was not explosive. The problem was that the income per head of the First World countries also continued to grow, so that on average, apart from Japan, there was no significant catching up. (See Chart 4 on p. 19).

Then, from the mid-1980s onward (in the case of China, actually earlier) a number of countries, all in East Asia, demonstrated sharp take-off. In the '90s the rest of the Third World followed with a marked acceleration of growth, and in a few cases, such as Uganda, the rate was explosive – 5 to 8 per cent per annum – as compared to the new improved rates in South Asia and Latin America – typically 4 per cent.

At one time the explosive-growth conundrum had seemed like old beliefs about cultivating parsley. You must do this, you must not do that and maybe the seed will germinate; maybe it won't. If it does germinate, the plants may wither, but maybe they won't. Then, if they do not wither, the herb will grow ferociously like a weed, and you will have more than you know what to do with.

Now we know that some of the advice on growing parsley seed, like preparing the bed with boiling water, is worse than useless. So also were some national development policies pursued in the past. But in the twenty-first century, it looks as if it will be increasingly possible to be confident that when a country effectively follows certain procedures, it will take off. The technology is there, but will it be used?

Economic growth in the Third World is a process of industrialization. The people are drawn into industry from agriculture without reducing the output of food. The essential requirements are therefore agricultural rationalization, industrial entrepreneurship, business organization and the savings and investment needed for infrastructure and industrial capacity. Somehow the economy and society has to be transformed from one which is growing slowly, and saving and investing only a small proportion of its total income, to one where saving, investment and growth are doubled or trebled.

In the early stages of development studies, attention was concentrated on economic questions. How much new capital was needed for a given amount of growth? How could a poor country save more? How much help could come from overseas? More recently, much more attention has been paid to the underlying social and political factors that may impede the economic transformation. A wide range of factors has been suggested, not all consistent with one another. There are, however, few experts who would now disagree that the essential ingredients of the recipe of take-off, anywhere in the Third World, are *culture, education* and *effective government*. Of course the ingredients interact. Education affects culture, and culture affects attitudes to education. Good government depends on both and also reinforces both.

The Role of Culture

The classic first observations on culture were made in relation to the First World in the early part of the twentieth century by the German sociologist Max Weber and then by the British historian R.H. Tawney. They saw what has since been confirmed over and again – that there has been a strong connection between business enterprise and the Protestant version of Christianity. In Germany, where there are both Protestantism and Catholicism, Weber was able to show that the great business families were overwhelmingly Protestant. He attributed the phenomenon to the social and psychological effects of the Calvinist doctrine of predestination. The ultimate fate of a person's soul was predetermined at birth. Until one died one could not know one's fate, but business success during life would be an encouraging sign. Tawney's explanation lay on the other side of the coin, that is, in Catholic theology which in the past had made a sin of 'usury' – lending money at interest. Neither explanation is convincing: the predestination doctrine, surely, is more likely to discourage than encourage general motivation and it is known that even in the Middle Ages Christians found many ways of getting round the anti-usury doctrine.

More recently the brilliant Harvard economic historian, David Landes in his book *The Wealth and Poverty of Nations* (1998) has suggested a more complex interaction between religious and temporal authoritarianism – resistance to change, resistance to popular government, resistance to scientific explanation, resistance to innovation in general. For example, although the Christian scriptures have little to say on the subject, in the fifteenth century the Church put Galileo on trial for supporting the theory that the earth went round the sun. After being shown instruments of torture, the great scientist recanted and was kept under house-arrest for the rest of his life. It has been said that, as a result, scientific inquiry in southern Europe came to a halt for the next two centuries.

Whatever the explanation, it was still the case in the middle of the twentieth century, and even later, that the average income per head of First World countries where the Catholic Church, the state and the society were or had been locked in a strong general traditionalist embrace, was lower by as much as 50 per cent than the average in the other First World countries. The argument that the great economic success of the United States was at heart the result of combining bountiful natural resources with the human energies of the Protestant Christian culture, however unpopular, is patently correct.

Since the 1960s, major First World countries or regions that were once Catholic and traditionalist, but have become socially modernized, have taken off into rapid economic growth. This applies to Spain and northern Italy, for example, but not to southern Italy. After the main part of the island of Ireland became independent of Britain in the 1921, the country languished for more than half a century in a Catholic traditionalist economic backwater: as late as the middle '70s income per head was only half the average level in the Protestant regions of western Europe. In fact, on economic criteria, Ireland at that time could well have been classed as Third World. Since then the Republic elected its first woman president, and Irish society has become increasingly modernized. Church attendance has fallen rapidly as has the supply of recruits for the priesthood. After an early setback, a take-off into rapid economic growth has occurred and the gap between Ireland's income per capita and that of the rest of Europe has substantially narrowed and appears to be continuing to do so.

As a result of colonization, which David Landes graphically describes in his book, the shadow of the traditionalist-Catholic ethic is still to be seen in the Third World. That cultural tradition is surely a major explanation of the dramatic difference in long-run performances of North and South America. The richest Latin American country today is Argentina. In 1900 she had income per capita only one-third below the United States; by the year 2000 that gap will have doubled. Over the whole of the second half of the twentieth century, income per head in Brazil grew at less than $2^1/2$ per cent per annum. As a result, Brazil today has an even lower per capita income than Argentina, one of the most unequal income distributions in the world and fifty million people in absolute poverty. The same story also surely explains the past economic backwardness of French Canada, where the culture was until recently much more Catholic and much more traditionalist than in the mother country, France.

Finally there is one East Asian country that has 'escaped' both the rapid growth and the late '90s financial crisis, namely the Philippines, originally colonized by Spain and still strongly traditionalist-Catholic. The Philippines have a lower average income per head and a much higher proportion of people in absolute poverty than the corresponding averages for the whole of the rest of East Asia. In fact, the general social, economic and political profile of the Philippines looks more like that of a Latin American than an East Asian country.

In addition to the classic story of the Catholic ethic, there is evidence that other religions, particularly Hinduism, have a similar effect when followed in a strong traditionalist context, as in the more backward subregions of India for example. At least this is the author's interpretation of the graphic description of traditionalist causes of Indian regional backwardness by Jean Drèze and Amartya Sen in their excellent book on Indian development, *The Political Economy of Hunger* (1997): 'Uttar Pradesh [in the north east] remains one of the most backward states in India, and, had this state of 140 million people been an independent country, it would have been not only one of the largest, but also one of the most socially deprived countries in the world.' It is surely not a coincidence that traditional Hinduism, strongly linked to the social-caste system, is particularly prominent in this state.

The other side of the story is the culture of the Orient. First Japan, then East Asian countries under strong ethnic Chinese influence and then China itself took off. Nobody can doubt the force that exists at the turn of the twentieth and twenty-first centuries in the Chinese business culture. (That of Japan may be experiencing a loss of drive brought on by maturity.) Until the Far Eastern financial crisis, which began in 1997, fast sustained growth-rates of income per head and major poverty reduction were achieved throughout the region. The financial crisis was, in fact, the product of the fast growth itself, the result of the real economies running ahead of their financial infrastructure.

The conclusion is that different cultures encourage or discourage economic growth. In the Third World, failure to grow implies failure to reduce poverty. In the First World, while the adverse effect of traditionalist-Catholic culture on growth was obvious, at least in the past, the effect on poverty was less so. As successive Papal encyclicals have shown, the Catholic tradition often shows a more explicit moral concern about excessive economic inequality than have the non-Catholic or 'Protestant' traditions. This has had significant social consequences for 1990s economic and social history in the continental west European as compared to the Anglo-Saxon countries, which will be discussed in Chapter 6.

It is also apparent that the effect of culture is far from immutable. It can, in fact, change quite rapidly. But change requires leadership.

The Role of Education

The role of education, most especially primary education, is increasingly understood. Secondary and higher education are also important, but a highly educated elite cannot make a proper economic contribution if the mass of the population remains illiterate or nearly illiterate. The process of advance depends uniquely on the economic co-operation of different kinds of labour and talents. Primary education for women is also of major importance in fostering a rational approach to family-planning and generally challenging traditionalism.

Although education costs money, provision of universal primary education need not be an insupportable burden on poor countries. Some poor countries or poor sub-regions (the famous case is the Indian state of Kerala) achieve high rates of enrolment in primary education and of adult literacy. In Africa south of the Sahara, adult literacy rates vary from 20 per cent to 80 per cent. North of the Sahara the case of Egypt, however, teaches the lesson that no one ingredient in the recipe for successful development dominates the others: Egypt's primary education statistics are slightly worse than India's, yet Egypt has higher average income per head than India.

Drèze and Sen suggest that in Uttar Pradesh the primary education situation is considerably worse even than the official statistics suggest. Apparently the enrolled children are often not being taught because the teachers are absent moonlighting (or rather 'daylighting') in other money-earning activities. They discover a whole culture of apathy towards primary education, from bottom to top of the society.

The ineffective state government reflects, they suggest, a basic elitist attitude which is more interested in producing professors than skilled workers. In the introductory chapter of their book, they suggest that the whole of India suffers from an elitism founded in traditional Hinduism. They also to some extent blame Islam, comparing the attitude to education of both religions unfavourably with that of Buddhism. It is certainly true that by Third World standards illiteracy is exceptionally low in Sri Lanka, Thailand and Burma.

The fundamental implication of the discoveries of Drèze and Sen is that effort in relation to primary education is as much a matter of attitude as of money. This has the crucial further implication that a very large improvement in the overall performance of the Third World in primary education, and hence a large increase in the global rate of poverty reduction, could be achieved without major extra cost simply by more effective government. But government behaviour also reflects public attitudes, which in turn reflect culture.

The Role of Government

This leads us to the actual role of government. The key word is effective. Whether the system of a country is democratic or authoritarian, it is essential that the political leadership is genuinely devoted to the cause (that is, the cause of economic growth and poverty reduction), and understands that this must be backed up by administrative action, and also requires the support of the people. It is difficult enough to manage a rational economic policy in a First World country, but the enormous handicaps under which Third World politicians labour make it all the more difficult. But politicians are in principle elected for no other purpose than to help their people. There is no other legitimate aim to the profession of politics. In many Third World countries, especially in the past, undemocratic leaders have seemed mainly interested in power for its own sake. In others, as in India, where the democratic process has been basically sustained, there has been political apathy towards development problems. There have also been heroic efforts, however, increasingly with results, by particular ministers and administrators. Manmohan Singh, economics and finance minister in New Delhi, is generally hailed as an outstanding example and it is widely believed that the upturn in the Indian growth path, noticeable since the early '90s, has been very much due to the results of his policies.

The Role of Policy

In that connection, a major issue has turned on the question of 'protected' versus 'open' development policy. The first is associated with trying to build industries behind protective walls of tariffs and import quotas, while also pursuing a strongly government-interventionist domestic policy, including state ownership of some industries. The second is associated with more liberal imports, a competitive foreign exchange rate and a general policy of encouraging domestic industrialization by encouraging the expansion of exports based on the foundation of the 'competitive' (in other words, cheap) price of labour in the Third World as compared to the First World. There is general agreement that the protective policy was not successful, and it has been widely transformed into a more 'open' policy, most dramatically in India. There is also wide agreement that the poor of the world will not be helped if the free-market philosophy is carried to extremes. As well stated in another quotation from the British Government White Paper of 1997, a balance is required:

> There have been two flaws in models of development over the past half-century. The first was characterized by a belief that the State should extend its control over production and trading activities, and over the allocation of resources and prices, in a way which created distortions and led to inefficiency and corruption. The second was a belief in a minimalist State and unregulated market forces which failed to secure economic growth . . . . There is now an opportunity to create a new synthesis which builds on the role of the State in facilitating economic growth and benefiting the poor. Both the State and markets make good servants and bad masters. We have learned that the virtuous State has a role to play in supporting economic developments which encourage human development and stimulate enterprise . . . .

It is significant that in China, for the past twenty years, the non-democratic government has been officially committed to a Marxian ideology. But Chinese government economic policy has in reality been highly pragmatic. There has been continuous experiment with 'hybrid' forms of organization which through decentralization provide local leaders and managers with incentives to efficiency, while yet keeping ultimate ownership of 'the means of production' (that is, business property) in public hands. A vigorous private sector has also grown up, albeit within a yet ambiguous framework of property rights.

The 'Chinese compromise' has both a bad aspect and a good one. The bad aspect is that the ambiguities concerning the ownership of business property mean that decisions of great commercial significance to third parties are made by individual bureaucrats. The result, inevitably, is corruption, a traditional problem in China, and in the 1990s giving increasing cause for concern. The good aspect is that in the debates that go along with 'democratic centralism' (discussion followed by consensus followed by conformity) there appears a permanent awareness that the purpose of development is the reduction of poverty. This is an important reminder in a society where an inevitable and not discreditable effect of take-off has been the emergence of a private business class whose obvious priority is making money.

The test of the pudding is in the eating. Although there may be some doubt as to how fast productivity and income is actually increasing in the Chinese rural sector (but does any other country in the world have a television channel devoted to programmes about peasant agricultural techniques?), the growth explosion in the industrial and urban sectors is obvious to all. Although Chinese growth may slow down, the basic path does appears sustainable.

One hopes that, following the recent acceleration, take-off will also occur in South Asia. The fate of a billion poor people depends on South Asian countries continuing to develop growth-effective government hopefully within the framework of political democracy.

CHAPTER 5

THE ROLE OF AID

For the best part of half a century, political leaders and thinking citizens in the First World have acknowledged concern about the extreme international disparity of economic welfare by supporting a permanent flow of money and technical assistance, loosely called 'development aid'. By the end of the 1960s most First World governments, including Japan, had created budgets and administrative structures (such as the British Ministry of Overseas Development founded in 1964 or the US Agency for International Development founded in 1963), for giving or lending money and experts on a 'bilateral' (state to state) basis to a large number of countries. The whole programme of bilateral aid is co-ordinated among the provider countries by a special committee of the OECD, an inter-government body originally named the 'Organization for European Economic Co-operation', which changed its name to 'Organization for Economic Co-operation and Development' in deference to the new priorities. In Britain, some very distinguished politicians Barbara Castle, Chris Patten and Clare Short – have held this ministerial responsibility. In the United States, Hollis Chenery, world-famous Harvard development economist, held a corresponding post, and subsequently became World Bank Director responsible for economic development research and policy.

The International Bank for Reconstruction and Development (IBRD, now known as 'The World Bank'), originally founded for post-war reconstruction, soon became exclusively concerned with Third World development. In the last two decades of the century, along with other international bodies, such as the United Nations Standing Conference on Trade and Development, the Bank has increasingly emphasized that poverty reduction is the essential aim of development policy – an approach which was, in fact, pioneered by Hollis Chenery. In the mid-1990s another world-famous US economist, Joseph Stiglitz, then Chairman of President Clinton's Council of Economic Advisers, became the World Bank's Chief Economist. There are also regional models of the World Bank. And finally, and most importantly, the United Nations Development Programme is supported by cash grants from First World UN members for a large world-wide programme of Technical Assistance.

The World Bank borrows money in First World markets to lend to Third World governments for development projects. Because the loans are in effect collectively guaranteed by the First World governments, the terms are substantially cheaper than those that many of the recipient governments could obtain on their own. In addition, the World Bank organizes an International Development Association to solicit cash grants from First World member governments for the purpose of subsidizing the terms of loans (called 'soft loans') to the poorer Third World countries.

The Structure of Aid

When the cash provided by individual provider governments is pooled into an entity such as the World Bank, which then selects projects to fund in recipient countries, the aid is called 'multilateral'. All money flowing directly or indirectly from individual governments in the form of bilateral or multilateral aid is called 'official' aid. About a third of all official aid is multilateral.

The First World also takes credit for so-called 'private flows' – that is, when a private individual or non-government entity (a firm or a bank, for example) invests money in a developing country by buying newly issued government or private bonds or shares, or by transferring profits into overseas branches or subsidiaries. Aid is usually measured as a 'net flow', meaning the total amount of cash going out in grants, loans and investments, *less* the return flow of debt interest, debt repayments and profits.

In 1990, the general scale of net official aid on the one hand and net private flows on the other was about equal, but in the following five years there was a large increase in private flows, while official aid stayed constant. In the year before the East Asian financial crisis of late 1997, the scale of private flows had become three times that of the official flows.

The Scale of Aid

By the year 2000 the total GDP of the First and Third Worlds, when calculated to correct differences in domestic price levels, will be approximately equal. Assuming only modest inflation in the last years of the century, the two figures will both be around twenty trillion (twenty thousand billion) US dollars. The difference is, of course, that the twenty trillion dollars in the First World will be produced by three quarters of a billion people, while the Third World's twenty trillion will be produced by five billion people. Conveniently this means that a given amount of aid represents about the same percentage of the total GDP of the provider countries as that of the recipient countries. Thus, superficially, the economic burden to the providers is equal in weight to the benefit to the recipients. In reality, of course, because the citizens of the Third World are so much poorer, their benefit in economic welfare is very much greater than the corresponding cost, in welfare, to the providers.

Official Aid

At the end of the twentieth century the total net flow of official aid (multilateral plus bilateral) is between fifty and sixty billion US dollars a year. That is, between a third and a half of one per cent of the GDP on both sides. This amounts to three to five US cents per day for each member of the Third World population. These calculations, however, are a rather gloomy way of looking at the situation. Increasingly, as already discussed, official aid is aimed at the Third World population in absolute poverty. The world poverty table (p. 27) showed us that the Third World poverty population is just over a quarter of the Third World total population. If as an extreme and rather unrealistic assumption one imagined that all official aid was successfully directed to the poverty population, then the figure of three to five cents a day becomes ten to twenty cents a day. Ten cents and twenty cents are not insignificant proportions of $1 a day. By the same token, official aid can be calculated to be at least 10 per cent of the poverty population's total income (GDP), again a significant figure. Of course, this way of doing the calculation exaggerates the anti-poverty impact of official aid, but it serves to underline the enormous significance of aid that is tied to actual poverty-reduction projects and programmes. The World Bank, the United Nations Development Programme and the British government (since the election of a new administration in 1997) are in the forefront of the movement to make official aid work this way.

Thirty per cent of official aid goes to Asia, 70 per cent to the rest of the Third World. Asia, however, has 40 per cent of the total Third World population. The region's official aid per head of population is therefore considerably lower than the average. The reason for this is a phenomenon that has been an apparently inexorable feature of official aid ever since the programme began: small countries tend to get more per head than large countries. The average population of a typical aid-receiving country in Asia is about 200 millions. In the rest of the Third World the figure is about 20 millions.

Why? Small countries are by no means necessarily on average poorer than large countries. India, one of the largest countries, is also one of the poorest. The answer is essentially political. Official aid goes to governments and, almost by definition, every aid-receiving country has a government of some kind (if it didn't, it would receive no aid). The administrators of both bilateral and multilateral aid like to spread their dealings over their 'clients'. Every potential recipient government, however small the population of its country, is a potential client and lobbyist. It is (allegedly) difficult to award less than a minimum amount. If the total amount of world official aid were re-distributed to give Asian countries shares in fair proportions to their populations, the amount left over for the rest of the world, *per country*, would be so small as to be (allegedly) politically embarrassing. As a result the poor people of large poor countries get much less help than the poor people of poor small countries. This helped the poor of Africa, but hurts the poor of India. Undoubtedly, the total poverty-reducing impact of the world aid programme is thus seriously weakened.

There is a United Nations target that every First World country should devote just under three quarters of one per cent of their GDP to net official aid. No large country approaches this, but in the '60s and '70s the British figure averaged a respectable figure not much below one half of one per cent, reaching a peak, in fact, in 1979, when Mrs Thatcher was first elected. Thereafter the figure fell progressively for five years, after which it stabilized at around half the previous level. Soon after the new British government took office in 1997, the White Paper *Eliminating World Poverty* was published, stating:

> We are committed to reversing the decline in the British [aid] budget and to the UN target.... This year and next we have said that we will work within the existing ceilings while conducting a comprehensive review to ensure that all our resources are effectively used.... Having done so we can justify increasing our development assistance budget from 1999/2000.

Since then the government announced general expenditure plans involving a major long-term increase in aid, which will eventually restore a significant part of the previous reductions.

Private Flows

In the mid-1990s total net private flows from the First to the Third World were running at $250 billion a year, almost four times the total of official aid. It has not always been so. Private flows fluctuate with market sentiment and follow success and failure. At the beginning of the 1990s, private flows amounted to less than official aid. At that time they were still depressed by the set-backs of the previous decade, particularly in Latin America. It is highly likely that the East Asian crisis at the end of the decade will cause yet another fluctuation. The crisis was exacerbated by exchange-rate instability, the result of general instability of the world financial system.

For obvious reasons, private flows are not aimed specifically at the poor, but they contribute to general economic growth. At its height in the mid-1990s they represented $1^1/_2$ per cent of the total GDP of the Third World. More significantly, they were about 20 per cent of the Third World's capital requirements for growth.

One can turn that figure around. Allowing for official aid, one can say that no less than *three-quarters* of the Third World's capital requirements are, and have to be, created at home.

The Critique of Bilateral Aid

There is a widely held view that bilateral aid, which is tied to being spent in the provider country, is so distorted to commercial interests – in effect, the argument goes, it is just an export subsidy – that its value to the recipient country is reduced to almost nothing. Although this view has some force, and although there are notoriously bad examples, like the British–Malaysian Pergau Dam project – it is also exaggerated. The salary of an expert sent out to establish, say, a school of printing is entirely paid by the provider government. In order to attract applicants the salary package, rightly or wrongly, needs to contain generous 'expatriate' allowances. Maybe most of this person's total remuneration will stay in a bank in the home country and only a small part is spent locally, with the result that very little actual cash travels from provider to recipient country. But if the project succeeds and a school of printing is not only established but continues to function effectively after the expert returns home, the recipient country has gained a real benefit. It now has a valuable piece of infrastructure for which it has paid nothing. Of course, if the project had not been tied, the contract could have been thrown open to all-comers, and a better or cheaper expert might have been hired. But that is both a speculative and secondary effect.

The British White Paper shows substantial sympathy for the critics of tied aid and states that the government will press for greater untying of official aid in the international arena of policy-making. But they do not propose to untie British aid at a faster rate than other provider countries. Instead they hope to employ the leverage of tied aid to foster good government and anti-poverty economic development.

The Final Assessment

Would there be a sharp and sustainable increase in Third World economic growth and poverty reduction if there were a massive increase in official aid? It is no answer to say that the event is politically unlikely. The human spirit, though often irrational, is not totally so. Whether something is politically likely is at least partly affected by the judgment of its costs and benefits.

In any given phase of a country's economic development there is almost certainly an upper limit on the amount of externally financed resources the country can usefully absorb. It is very difficult to suppose, however, that if the current world total of official aid were doubled, and thus brought nearer the UN target, there would be any significant difficulty of 'absorption'.

A major increase in official aid would, therefore, make a significant contribution to the reduction of world poverty. This is, however, neither a necessary nor a sufficient condition for the success of the programme to eliminate poverty. The greater part of the resources of human and material capital must inevitably come from inside the Third World itself.

For example, if the First World countries desired to reduce to zero the number of people in the Third World who have no safe water by means of a ten-year programme of sewage works, they could collectively provide official aid capital grants over a period of ten years and then maintenance grants starting at 100 per cent of cost and tapering down to zero over twenty years. They could finance this by an increase in the general burden of taxation on the richest 20 per cent of their own population initially representing no more than 2 per cent of these people's income in the first year, which would have fallen to one per cent twenty years later. Since the average per capita income of this group of people is at least $100 a day, they would initially be sacrificing the enormous sum of $2 a day!

One retort from opponents could well take the form of the interesting calculation that the same programme could be fully financed by comparable taxation levied on the richest 20 per cent of the population of the Third World. Although of course the richest fifth of the population of the Third World earns at best $10 (adjusted for cost of living), rather than $100 a day. By the same token because they are so much more numerous their per capita contribution would be much smaller – measured in cents rather than dollars. Why, it could be argued, should they not contribute?

A highly attractive proposal would be a joint scheme in which the cost of eliminating bad water throughout the whole world within a period of ten to twenty years would be shared equally between the richest 20 per cent of the populations of the First and Third Worlds. What an exciting project that would be. Strangely, although very many people, especially in the First World, deplore the general water-supply situation in the Third World, no one else, to the author's knowledge, has put such a project forward. The simple figures quoted, however, cannot be gainsaid. The most obvious objection likely to be put forward, of course, would be that the project would compete for funds with the general programme of official aid. That would depend, however, on whether or not it could be successfully organized not as yet another tax-financed project, but rather as an independent global charity, to which people would divert this tiny amount from their general expenditure. In the last analysis, it is, as always, a matter of priorities. Finally, of course, there could well be resistance from Third World governments not wishing to concede the realities of their domestic situations.

Such apparent obstacles to an apparently desirable project again illustrate the basic and central theme of this book, namely that the obstacles to reducing human poverty are mainly to be found not in shortages of money, resources or technology, but in various forms of human obtuseness.

Chapter 6

The New Poor

It is a quite extraordinary and deeply disturbing fact that in the last quarter of the twentieth century, when general prosperity abounded, the First World countries have themselves become more, rather than less, troubled by poverty.

In the halcyon days of the 1960s, the bottom fifth of the population in both Britain and the USA were doing historically well. Not only was average income per head in the whole society rising briskly, but the bottom groups were doing better than the average. As a result British families in this income group could expect that even if their children did not rise in the social scale they would nevertheless enjoy over their lifetimes nearly double the living standard of their parents. In the USA the same thing was happening, although less strongly. Not only were millions of people coming out of absolute poverty every year, but relative deprivation was also falling steadily.

In the USA things first began to go wrong in the early 1970s. The growth of the economy slowed down, and the share of the poorest 20 per cent stopped increasing: at the end of the decade they were absolutely no better off than at the beginning. Ten years later they were still there. In fact until the late '90s (and on some evidence not even then), the worst-off fifth of the US population, numbering twenty-five million, had had no increase in their standard of living for thirty years.

In the UK, however, not only the absolute income but also the relative share of the group continued to rise, with the result that both kinds of poverty continued to fall. In 1979, the relative share reached the record level of 10 per cent and the absolute income per head was now no less than twice what it had been a quarter century earlier and no less than three times what it had been at the outbreak of World War II. The group had come to a position where their cash income net of tax, adjusted for international cost-of-living differences, was only a fifth below that of their US counterparts. After taking account of other benefits, such as the health service, the welfare level of low-income Brits was almost certainly at least equal to that of low-income Americans. In sharp contrast, the richest 20 per cent of British were no less than two-thirds below the richest Americans. At that time, at the bottom end of the income distribution, Britain was a very much less unequal country than the USA. Of course, Britain's average (real) income per head was still well below that of the USA, but because the difference in inequality works in the other direction, the transatlantic difference of Social Welfare was significantly less that the raw income figures would allow.

Then, almost overnight, in the year 1980, disaster struck the unskilled branch of the British working class. Inside three years, their living standard (real income per head of the worst-off 20 per cent) fell absolutely by more than a fifth. During the rest of the '80s and early '90s some ground was recovered, but in the mid-'90s it was still the case that the group was absolutely no better off than fifteen years earlier. Thus, as in the USA, so in the UK: while the top classes made large gains, the poorest class stood still. Had the prosperity of the British poorest class continued to gain at the average rate of the previous quarter century, instead of coming to a halt after 1979, their standard of living in the year 2000 would have been approximately double the level that is now likely to be the case.

On the European continent, the main problem was rising unemployment spread quite broadly over the social classes. During the early '90s, the general unemployment rate in the former West Germany rose to 8 per cent, in the late '90s to 12 per cent. (In contrast, in the USA the figure had come down to 5 per cent and in the UK to 6 per cent.) The welfare system on the continent of Europe is quite strong and so also is minimum wage legislation. As a result, the increase in unemployment did not result in a major increase in absolute poverty or income inequality. Deprivation came in the form of exclusion from the work force ('social exclusion', as described by the European Union), especially among people under the age of 25 and most especially among young women. In France, in the mid-'90s, the official unemployment rate among women aged 20–25 was no less than 30 per cent, but among women aged 30–35 it was as low as 8 per cent. In effect, work was being 'rationed'.

The Scourge of Unemployment

In Britain, 1979 saw the election of a government committed to strong reductions of taxes on the rich. This suggests that perhaps the main explanation lay there: if the rich are taxed less, in one way or another the poor must be taxed more. But although these tax changes did occur, they are not the main answer: the historical story is basically similar whether one uses before or after tax statistics.

So what else was happening on a large scale in the USA around 1970 and in the UK a decade later that could be an obvious immediate cause of a sudden large increase in poverty? Unlike the case of western Europe, the answer was unemployment. From the end of World War II to the end of 1970, the American official unemployment rate had never risen above 7 per cent, and had averaged, in fact, around $4^1/2$ per cent. In Britain the average figure was $1^1/2$ per cent and the peak figure no more than $2^1/2$ per cent!

In the five years immediately after 1970, US unemployment lurched upwards, downwards and then further upwards, first reaching a peak of $8^1/2$ per cent in 1976, then falling quite sharply but almost immediately taking off again to reach, in 1982, a post-World War II record of 10 per cent.

The pattern was virtually the same after 1980 in Britain. In the previous three years the British unemployment rate had crept up somewhat – to the terrible (as it then seemed) level of 5 per cent! Between 1979 and 1982 the figure jumped from there to 10 per cent, and was still rising. For the next fifteen years the British total unemployment rate averaged $8^1/2$ per cent, and over half the period it reached double figures. In fact, the rate dipped significantly only once – during the ill-fated economic boom of the late '80s: at its lowest then, at 6 per cent, it was twice the highest figure ever reached in Britain after World War II and before 1980. And, as we have also already seen, even more obviously than in the USA, the timing of the explosion of unemployment was tightly linked to the onset of the income disaster of the unskilled working class. Surely the relation of cause and effect is obvious?

By the mid-'80s US unemployment had come down quite considerably, and for ten years afterwards fluctuated between 5 and $7^1/2$ per cent, compared with corresponding pre-1970 figures of between $3^1/2$ and 6 per cent. In the second half of the '90s, there was a further significant improvement as the US economy seemed to move towards a general condition of 'full employment'. There was also eventual recovery in the UK, with the rate at the end of the '90s falling to almost as low as the US figure. But British unemployment had overtaken that of the USA long before in 1982, and since then, up to the time of this book going to press, that relationship has never reversed. It is significant that the adverse *change* of economic inequality was, as we have seen, much sharper in Britain than America.

In addition to unemployment, there is 'non-participation' – those who are not working but are not classified as unemployed because there is no direct evidence that they are actively seeking work. The unemployed plus the non-participants make up the total of the 'non-employed'. Their percentage in the corresponding total population of working age is called the 'non-employment rate'. In both countries, among males, this rate doubled in the twenty years after 1970. Among males with only a basic education, it quadrupled, and in the year 2000 it may still be the case in both Britain and the USA that one in four of all low-educated males will not be working. Fortunately, as a result of the revolution in educational participation, this group is a steadily declining proportion of the corresponding population – 20 per cent in the UK and 15 per cent in the US, compared to figures three times as high in the '70s. A major element in the 'new poverty' are the people who, for one reason or another, the educational revolution left behind.

The Dark Heart

So what are the non-employed, especially the long-term, non-participating non-employed, doing? How are they surviving? Some had unemployment benefit or other welfare support, but others did not. The answer has to be that they are scraping by in one way or another; grey or black market paid work; thieving, begging; drug dealing; or receiving help from friends and relatives. In the USA, at least 3 per cent of all prime-age males with only a primary education is 'non-employed' by virtue of being in prison. This is a significant chunk of total non-employment. Although black people are massively over-represented in the US prison population, the imprisonment rate among whites is also high. A quarter of all the people in US prisons are there for drug offences. If drug offences did not exist and blacks were not over-represented, the US crime and prison picture would not be so very different from that of other countries. But as things are, the total US imprisonment rate is five times higher than in any other country in the world. At the same time that US society has created millions of new jobs for qualified men and women, it has added three quarters of a million of mostly unqualified males, and especially black people, to the prison population. Whether or not a person deserves to be in prison, once there, as recently graphically described by Howard Marks (*Mr Nice*, 1997) they obviously suffer capability deprivation. That in fact is their punishment. It is clearly a form of poverty. Of course, the majority of the non-employed are not in prison. But there is overwhelming evidence that a high proportion are in poverty.

A path-breaking book *The Dark Heart* (1997) provided a searing picture of real life in what the author Nick Davies described as 'hidden Britain'. He graphically narrates searing personal histories of prostitution, burglary, violence, drug dealing, absolute poverty and mental depression. He asks why a world of chaos and violence is suddenly pumping out increasing numbers of deeply damaged people. 'Is it that this world is a new creation? Or is it an old world which has changed?' His basic answer is the collapse of jobs. Writing of a community called Hyde Park in Leeds, Yorkshire, he says:

> During the 1980s this community was shaken to its foundations by a series of massive quakes as the underlying structure of work shifted and splintered . . . . The Screw Company, the forge, the brewery, all the old textile plants and engineering firms were either cut or closed for ever.

It was as if someone had drilled a hole in the underside of Hyde Park and drained away its jobs . . . . The material hardship which then settled over the community was clear.

Many employed people in the First World are also in poverty. Their annual earnings are insufficient to support themselves and their families above the poverty line. Mostly they are people with few or only weak educational or vocational qualifications. People with below average IQ scores are also strongly represented, as they are too among the prison population and the non-imprisoned non-employed population of prime-age males. During precisely the same historical periods (after 1970 in the USA and after 1980 in the UK) in which unemployment rose and the real income of the worst-off fifth of the total population stagnated, the inflation-adjusted average hourly wages of unskilled or less-skilled workers either declined absolutely (in the case of the USA) or failed to grow (in the case of the UK). In other words, what went wrong in the two economies affected both employed and non-employed. Essentially it was a general problem for all the people on the wrong side of the fence as regards the parents and brains they inherited and the education they are able to acquire. Why?

The reason is extremely simple. Sudden increases in open unemployment such as occurred in the '70s and '80s in the USA and the UK can only mean that the general demand for labour fell relatively to the supply. (The answer cannot be on the 'supply side' because changes there happen only relatively slowly.) The immediate effect is the rise in open unemployment. After that there are two consequential effects: a rise in general non-employment and a fall in average wages as some of the people who have lost their jobs find new but lower-paid ones. Both the rise in non-employment and the fall in wages are consequences of the first cause, which is the failure of the economy to sustain an adequate general level of demand for labour. Inevitably, those who suffer most are those whose economic bargaining position is already fragile, that is, the unskilled, less-skilled and less-educated members of the workforce.

Why Did It Happen?

The rise in poverty in the First World was connected with the fall in the labour market. Why, then, after a quarter of a century of prosperity, did the market for less-skilled workers on both sides of the Atlantic, collapse? The answer is quite controversial but (as the present author argued in *How to Save the Underclass*, 1996) the most obvious answer lies in the worldwide 'macro' economic turmoil which began in the early '70s, was reinforced in the early '80s and left an aftermath lasting until the early '90s. As well as a period of high unemployment, it was also a period of high inflation, the latter being an indirect cause of the former. Governments and monetary authorities faced almost impossible difficulties in managing their economies and believed they were compelled to let unemployment rise as a price of avoiding even worse inflation. In fact, rightly or wrongly, in so doing, they were also buying monetary stabilization at the expense of poverty. The short-run effect was the immediate fall in employment and rise in unemployment. The long-run effect was the slowing up of the general growth of the economy resulting in a cumulative tendency for job creation to fall behind labour supply.

At this point the reader is asked to turn back to the previous discussion of the fundamental relation between economic growth and job creation in the First World in Chapter 4 (pp. 47–48). First World leaders, and especially Britain's post 1997 'New Labour' leaders, are always searching for specific detailed and practical means to help people back to work. But over and again the public asks, 'What if the jobs aren't there?' If creeping non-employment and/or falling wages are to be avoided, the demand for labour must grow on average as fast as the supply of labour. Labour is needed to produce goods. Therefore the first requirement is that the economy's capacity to produce goods, and consumers' capacity to pay for them must be growing at a sufficient rate to match the supply. What elements make up the growth of the supply of labour? It is partly the natural growth of population, which in the UK and western Europe has become quite small. Far more important is the effect of the steadily increasing proportion of mothers who desire paid work. Even more important is the need for jobs to replace those lost through increased efficiency and techno-logical advance. Finally, on the other side of the coin, a deduction must be made for the historical downward trend (caused by affluence) in the average number of annual hours workers want to work. If this calculation is made for the major First World countries from 1970 onwards (in virtually every case a substantial cumulative deficit) it varies from 5 to 15 per cent of the prime-male labour force in relation to supply. As would be expected, these figures match the correspond-ing increases in non-employment.

Unfortunately, there is an influential though controversial argu-ment that the same factors which restrained poverty were also partly responsible for the increase in unemployment itself. This view, which is strongly supported by Britain's post-1997 'New Labour' govern-ment, claims that the European welfare system makes European labour too expensive to employ. It also claims that this explains why continental unemployment persisted.

Others (see, for example, B. Moss and J. Michie, *A Community in Crisis?* 1998) cite evidence that the persistent climb of continental west European unemployment is due to a general failure of the econo-mies to grow fast enough to create new jobs to replace those lost by organizational re-structuring and general productivity increases. In fact, several years of sustained economic growth are needed to work off the accumulated deficit in the labour market.

The most fundamental moral for First World anti-poverty policy is, therefore, 'Keep the economy growing'. The problem is, as Tony Blair stated when Opposition spokesman on the economy, it is not easy for a government to know how to achieve this. Be that as it may, if sufficient growth is not achieved, the basic problem of poverty will not be solved. For this reason we must, of course, return to the topic at the end of this book.

The Role of 'De-industrialization'

One important feature of the whole process can be seen in the words of Nick Davies. He described the basic problem as caused by a 'shifting and splintering' of the 'underlying structure of work'. He was referring not so much to the general loss of jobs but of particular kinds of jobs. They were industrial jobs for unskilled and semi-skilled men. Relatively to the skill required, they were well paid. They were in industries whose products were sold in what economists call 'oligopolistic' markets, meaning that there is brisk competition among a relatively small number of firms leaving room for good and quite secure profits. Represented by vigorous unions, workers could share the benefits of the situation because wage increases could generally be passed on to consumers. It was the classic situation of the 'blue-collar' working class in the First World from the time that labour unions first began to gain political and economic recognition in the first quarter of the twentieth century. It was a system that reached its peak in delivering the goods for workers (if not for consumers) somewhere around 1960. From then on, it was a system in decline.

Two factors wrought its destruction. The first was the tendency of affluent consumers to spend an increasing proportion of their incomes not on the products of industry, but on services. The service trades are very competitive and, because their products are labour intensive, they have little room for 'generous wages'. If a labour union succeeds in pushing up wages in a service industry, it is much more likely to drive away customers than is the case in industry. Service sector jobs are almost inevitably lower paid than industrial jobs.

The second factor was the opening up of international trade in industrial goods between the First World and the Third World. The First World at last let in from the Third World those industrial goods where the Third World had an advantage, namely those in which the prevailing techniques of production were comparatively labour intensive. In return, the Third World opened its markets to the more high-tech, low-labour goods of the First World. The benefit to the Third World was considerable: the changes in trade policy preceded the resumption of brisk general Third World growth which has already been described in Chapter 4. There were also great benefits to the consumers and general population in the First World. There was, however, one obvious group of losers: the less-skilled workers of the First World.

In time, it should be possible to manage this 'restructuring' of the world economy without too many cases of hardship. But if the original job losses happen very rapidly this will not be possible. The greater the speed of change the greater the proportion of people who will not be able to re-adjust in time. That was exactly the problem in Britain. Between 1978 and 1981 the pound sterling became a petrocurrency and rose so high on the world money markets that a whole swathe of British industry, especially located in the north and Midlands, became non-competitive overnight. For example, the author's family business, a public company listed on the Birmingham Stock Exchange, closed down after a hundred years of continuous trading.

Furthermore, faced with yet another outburst of world inflation, the British government instituted general deflationary policies. In 1979 when the Thatcher government was elected the general British unemployment rate was 4 per cent. Within eighteen months the figure had doubled and within three years it had nearly trebled. A major cause of poverty is, and always has been, not so much the nature of economic change, but its speed. The people who will suffer by waiting for the effects of slower change, consumers for example, have much less to lose than the people who will suffer hardship as a result of excessive speed.

The Role of Technology and Education

In addition to unemployment, non-employment and inadequate economic growth, the revolution caused by the new technology has exacerbated the situation – most especially the new information technology, which has burst upon us in the last two decades of the twentieth century and will be swirling all around us through most of the first half of the twenty-first century. It is an enormous total benefit to the human race, but seems to have a tendency to increase the inequality of earnings at all levels. Top managers are earning more relatively to middle managers, as are top secretaries relatively to bottom secretaries. The same may also be generally true, though not so obviously so, in respect of the relative earnings of 'white-collar' and 'blue-collar' jobs.

There has been a considerable discussion of the causes and effects of this phenomenon. Not all the effects necessarily go one way. If the operations of a warehouse employing a number of manual workers is computerized, the subsequent improvement in the efficiency of the deployment of labour has two potential effects with opposing implications. If the business cannot expand (because, maybe, the economy is not expanding) some workers may have to be let go. But the productivity of the remainder is enhanced – the firm can afford to pay higher wages without raising its selling prices. Whether the firm does actually raise wages depends on the general state of the labour market (and in some cases, of course, on the strength of unions). If the general labour market is booming, the firm will have to reward its employees for increased productivity or it will lose them. If it does, and if this is the general response of firms to this type of improvement, the new technology will not, finally, create much change in either direction in the overall extent of inequality. All that will happen (provided always that the general economy grows properly) is that the average standard of living of the whole population will rise.

But not all effects of the new technology are of this type. There is a persuasive but as yet only partly tested argument that the new technology tends to increase the earning power of those in the higher rungs of the economic ladder more than others. The economic system generates wealth by a general process of mass co-operation 'organized' by the hidden hand of the market. The productivity of one person affects the productivity of others. The work of 'top people' – hospital managers, head teachers, company executives – affects the productivity of a greater number of other people than does that of 'bottom' people. Consequently top people earn more.

The suggestion is that the new technology, by dramatically enhancing the processing of information has an especially strong effect on the efficiency of the functions of leadership, planning, supervision and control by which top people earn their keep. It has also been suggested that the new technology reduces the need for the specialization of functions within business firms and creates a relatively greater demand for people who are inherently versatile. The end result of all these ideas is that the new technology increases the relative market value of people who have the luck and ability to do jobs requiring versatility and/or leadership. Then, if the economic system continues to reward individuals, at least to some extent, according to their market abilities, there has to be some increase in the general inequality of earnings. The new technology will therefore yield a smaller gain in Social Welfare than would be indicated by the apparent gain in average productivity.

From this observation, many people, and most especially the British leaders of 'New Labour', have drawn the conclusion that the most important factor in avoiding the 'new poverty' is the educational system. It is impossible to deny the desirability of finding ways to improve the quality of the education not only made available, but also obtained, by the less-advantaged population. But there is an awkward body of evidence that the factor of inherited intelligence is also at work. If learning does not come easily, motivation is weakened and the temptation to drop out strengthened. Further, if one inherits from one's parents a below-average IQ, one is also more likely to have parents who give only weak support to one's motivation. This is part of the famous process by which class structures are created.

There is, in fact, strong evidence that even if a person is born into a family that is strictly average with respect to economic class but happens also to inherit a low performance ability in conventional verbal-reasoning tests administered around age seven, that person is more likely, to a very significant extent, to end up, at the age of thirty, in prison or in poverty out of prison.

If, as seems possible, we are here facing an inexorable process, which improvements in the educational system can ameliorate but not eliminate, it may be the case that some degree of long-run upward trend in general *pre-tax* inequality is inevitable. If society believes that, from the point of view of Social Welfare, something which is inevitable is also undesirable, the answer has to be an increase in redistribution via the tax system. In order to achieve the maximum benefit in terms of Social Welfare, the tax changes should of course be designed to minimize adverse effects on work incentives.

Poverty and the Welfare State

The system called the Welfare State, which actually developed gradually in the First World almost from the first decades of the twentieth century (culminating in the great development in the USA in the 1960s under President Lyndon Johnson) had only one basic objective, which was, of course, the reduction of poverty. To this end there was tax-paid support for unemployment, low wages, ill-health, disability, old age and other misfortunes. In respect of unemployment it was implicitly assumed that the economic system would generally be at full employment, so that when some people lost jobs others, most of the time, would be finding jobs. The system, therefore, was intended to finance a sharing of the burden of transition between the employed and the (hopefully temporarily) unemployed. Nobody imagined that the system could financially sustain a chronic situation of high general unemployment which would not only create permanent claims for unemployment benefits but also a general economic situation where more and more people would make valid claims for general income support, due to 'non-participation' in the labour force.

Until the mid-'70s, all went well. From then on the Welfare State has been battered by exactly the situation it could not sustain, that is, long-term massive unemployment rates. The most obvious effect is a permanent crisis of financing: income support takes up an ever-increasing share of tax revenues which could much better be devoted to other purposes (for example, health or education). A less obvious but much remarked additional effect has been so-called 'welfare dependency'. It is obvious that once general unemployment has become chronic, once people who never thought they would ever have to claim benefit have broken through that dismal barrier, the structure and attitudes of society must change. There will be increasing numbers of people for whom unemployment and non-employment have become a way of life. If and when the economy improves, these people will have been changed by their experience and may fail to go after the work that is available. A major effect of long-lasting large-scale unemployment is to increase the proportion of the population who appear to be 'work-shy'. It will not be the case that they will refuse all work, but it may be the case that they will need a strong financial incentive to be induced to work: it may seem as if they have withdrawn from the labour market. Thus high unemployment has an negative aftermath in the fight against poverty reduction. Inevitably, unemployment benefit that is not means-tested must run out. Thereafter, a person will have to find work, starve, or take up means-tested income support of one kind or another. What is available in the latter respect varies from country to country and also according to personal circumstances (for example, whether one is a parent of young children). But, no matter what the circumstances, once one has received means-tested income support, one has a built-in disincentive against resuming paid employment. It is not easy to design a tax and benefits system that avoids this. The reason is not technical. It is due to the simple logic that if a government eases the net taxation of additional income at the bottom level, it must either increase it at higher levels or suffer a loss of revenue. The same problem also affects schemes designed to ease the transition back into the labour market by subsidizing employers to take on previously unemployed workers.

By the middle of 1998, long-term unemployment in Britain had fallen to low levels; in south-east England, among able-bodied males, the long-term rate was down to one per cent. So convinced were they that a part of the population had become 'unemployable' (unemployable but yet employed!) that the Bank of England's Monetary Policy Committee decided that this low rate of long-term unemployment was a sign of impending inflation, and promptly raised interest rates. Critics claimed that the action would damage the real economy and cause a reversal of the downward trend of unemployment. Poor people who had recently acquired jobs would lose them again. This potentially unsettling effect on the conduct of policy is yet another example of the far-reaching adverse effects of the original outburst of unemployment – an aftermath of the aftermath.

The Basic Moral

So we see that finally we are back to the proposition with which we started. The basic cause of the new poverty has been failure of the 'macro' economic system. The basic way to reduce the new poverty is to forestall these kinds of failures in the future.

Good macro-economic management requires not only the maintenance of reasonable monetary stability (avoiding fast or accelerating inflation) but also maintaining low real interest rates and encouraging maximum possible economic growth. In this context, as the British experience after 1997 has shown, excessive monetary caution can be a serious mistake. Once inflation has been brought below around 3 per cent, the effects of straining to push it down further will tend to increase inequality and slow up long-term growth, inevitably adversely affecting Social Welfare. Unlike the case of the US Federal Reserve Board, the brief sent to the Bank of England when it was given 'independence' in 1997, referred only to inflation and said nothing of employment, unemployment, economic growth, poverty or Social Welfare. In March 1998 the Sunday *Observer* reported:

BLAIR'S NEW CHARTER FOR THE POOR
Minister's set themselves tough new targets to reduce:
Unwanted teenage pregnancies
Jobless families
Pensioners and children living in poverty

As the reader can see, there is no mention here of the economy. In the leading article of the same day, however, the newspaper commented, 'But if it is clever and strong politically, the Budget's economics are weaker . . . . Study after study has demonstrated that the key to employment creation is . . . the existence of a strong demand for labour. Work opportunities are not related to workers' willingness to work, but to employers' readiness to employ them.'

Prime Minister Blair did not respond. Some months later in a speech (30 July 1998) celebrating the first year's performance of his administration, he asked, 'What other government would have given financial independence to the Bank of England as well as setting up a unit to deal with homelessness?' What a strange apposition. Did he mean that he knew that the brief given to the Bank would compel it pursue policies that would necessarily tend to *increase* homelessness?

Misunderstanding of the role of macro-economic policy in the battle against poverty is not confined to any one segment of the political spectrum. In western Europe, at the end of the 1990s, it was, unfortunately, generally widespread through the political class. The European Central Bank which will determine monetary policy in the European Monetary Union will have a brief similar to that of the Bank of England.

The Problem in the Ex-Communist Countries

Leaving aside China, there are some twenty-five ex-Communist states, whose total population in the year 2000 will be about 7 per cent of the world population. They are called 'transition' countries because their economies are in transition from centrally planned socialism to market capitalism. The process began in the late 1980s and, although rapid, in the year 2000 will undoubtedly still be incomplete.

The UN, as we have seen, judges that $5 a day is an appropriate line for defining absolute poverty in all these countries. In other words, the UN judges that in order to live a reasonably decent life according to the previous history and prevailing standards (that is, in order to avoid capability deprivation) one needs four times the daily quantity of goods in Uzbekistan than in India, and between a quarter and a third of the quantity required in the United States, western Europe or Japan. On this standard, nearly a fifth of the whole population in the transition economies, or eighty million people, will be in absolute poverty in the year 2000 (as already shown in the table on p. 27 and discussed in Chapter 2). In contrast, the whole First World, with twice the population, and using the $15-a-day standard, will have fewer people in poverty.

This is a terrible tragedy. To varying degrees, both absolute and relative poverty have sharply increased in these countries (unlike any other region in the world) since the period immediately before the process of transition began. United Nations research has shown (*Poverty in Transition*, 1998) that, since average real income per capita has also declined sharply, Social Welfare has massively decreased. The story is not a good advertisement for capitalism. More precisely, it is a very bad reflection on the case for 'quick bang' transition. In Russia, the biggest bangs that can be heard seem to be the guns of gangsters who are said to have taken over the economy.

The extent of the disaster varies from country to country, and is clearly least in countries which did not become Communist until after World War II and who also, at that time, had relatively industrialized economies. In these countries, such as Hungary and the Czech Republic, absolute poverty has increased by about 15 per cent. Elsewhere the increase varies from 50 per cent to a 100 per cent.

There were five fundamental causes of the disaster. First and foremost, were the large absolute declines, ranging from 15 per cent to 50 per cent, in the total production of these economies, and a corresponding decline in average income per head. In the previous chapters of this book we have seen how brisk economic growth in the form of income per head is the key lever for *reducing* absolute poverty in the Third World. We have also seen how inadequate economic growth, in the form of total output, is liable to increase relative and even absolute poverty in the First World. But in the transition economies of the late 1990s, we are not speaking about 'inadequate' economic growth, we are speaking of massive negative growth. (There was negative growth in Latin America in the 1980s, but not on a comparable scale.) Inevitably, if average income per head declines absolutely, even if relative inequality does not increase, large numbers of people must be pulled down below the fixed absolute poverty line. These are people who were previously near to being poor. Now, with their real incomes reduced by anything up to a half, they are poor indeed.

The second factor flows from the first. It is always the case that when a disaster of this kind (such as the First World depressions of the early 1930s or '90s), the relatively poor suffer relatively more than the relatively rich. In other words general inequality increases. Consequently, not only is there an increase in relative poverty, but the upward pressure on absolute poverty is exacerbated. In the transition economies where the fall in production was less than 20 per cent, the rise in general inequality was generally modest: hence, in these economies the greater part of the increase in absolute poverty was due, in fact, to the fall in the national average living standard rather than to exacerbation by increased inequality. But in the countries, such as Russia and the Ukraine, where the fall in production was particularly great, the rise in general inequality was also great. Consequently, a large proportion of the increase in absolute poverty was due to increased inequality. The poor received a greatly reduced share of a greatly shrunken cake.

The third factor was a decline in the social services, caused in turn by disruption of the public finances. Under Communism the state financed all public expenditure, from defence to social services, from the profits of the whole of industry and the greater part of commerce, all these 'means of production' being, of course, under Communism, public property. In effect, there were few taxes, direct or indirect, in the sense understood in the First World. The state industries were subjected to a major levy called 'turnover tax' but this was basically no more than the instrument by which their profits were transferred to the centre. When the industries were 'privatized' this primary source of government revenue was lost and needed to be replaced by a conventional First World system of direct and indirect taxes. But such a system is not easily created, let alone accepted and effectively enforced overnight. Consequently all the public services, and with them all the social services, were severely squeezed.

The fourth factor was disorderly privatization. In truth, there does not really exist an orderly, just and legitimate process for rapidly converting a huge amount of public property into private property. In the First World, as a result of at least a thousand years of history, the mass of privately owned business property is held in clear legal title tested in long-established courts of law. With relatively few exceptions (for example, theft) each legal owner has acquired the title in a voluntary legal transaction of sale, gift or inheritance. If the previous transactions are traced back far enough, howver, there is usually an event of dubious legitimacy – in Britain following civil war or legalized sequestration of common lands, or in the United States following gunslinging skulduggery as the 'Wild' West (millions of acres of land, occupied by Native Americans but 'owned' by no one) was 'opened up'. But these origins are now buried in history. In contrast, the ex-Communist countries, urged on by First World advisors, are trying to collapse hundred-year processes into decades. The result, almost inevitably, has been ten years of *de facto* gangsterism. Through a variety of improvised processes, small groups of tough or lucky people, often the previous state managers, have ended up as the new owners – the new capitalists in post anti-capitalist society. Inevitably general economic inequality has thus further increased. Joseph Stiglitz (UNU/WIDER Annual Lecture, 1998) has character-ized the problem as a failure to distinguish between ownership and competition. Comparing Russia with China, he said, 'Russia has privatized a large fraction of its economy without doing much to promote competition. The contrast in performance could not be greater, with Russia's output below the level of almost a decade ago, while China has managed to sustain double-digit growth . . . .'

The fifth factor is the breakdown of general government. This is partly the result of the fourth factor but also the result of the obvious difficulty of fast transition to the conventions and practices of success-ful democratic government. In Russia, where there was virtually no previous experience of democracy of any kind (after the Revolution, a democratic system lasted only a few months before the Bolsheviks took over), the problem is at its worst.

The total result of these disasters is the creation of thirty million new poor. How long it may take for the benefits of political freedom and economic reform to outweigh these costs is yet unknown.

Why did general production decline? The whole purpose of reform was to increase, not reduce, economic efficiency. The answer is similar to and associated with the problem of fast privatization. It is not impossible, but it is not easy, to accelerate the growth of the institu-tions of a well-functioning market. The failures of government, the fiscal difficulties and the disorderly privatization process have all interacted to produce the basic overall economic disaster, that is, the decline in GDP. Other anti-poverty measures, such as the wider avail-ability of primary education, do not apply: Communism did effectively provide almost universal primary education and so far, except perhaps in the more remote Central Asian localities, that has held up. In Russia, secondary and higher education is also good, and the country has some of the best-qualified professionals in the world. While affluent First World citizens travel to Moscow for highly skilled special operations, the public health services decline.

All the various elements in the general problem of the 'transition' economies is vividly illustrated in the following quotation from a report on Mongolia:

> No Communist regime has experienced a more abrupt shift to a capitalist democracy than Mongolia . . . twelve times the size of England, with 30 million livestock, two and a half million people, and a most uncompromising free-market government. The animals are doing fine but many of the people are wondering whether the undiluted theories of Milton Friedman are really the answer . . . . In 1992 they were given vouchers that could be swapped for shares under the government's scheme to privatize everything . . . . The process, in practice, was riddled with corruption, but has produced a band of unlikely shareholders. The problem is that too many of these pilot capitalists do not have enough to eat. They have sold their shares for food. They say that compared to the socialist time, life is worse. They don't have any jobs, and must depend on the animals.'
>
> (*Independent*, London, August 1998)

The last sentence is significant. Previously the region had been heavily subsidized by Moscow. Now with independence and the subsidies gone, the people are back to where they were when socialism first arrived seventy years earlier: the harsh life of the nomadic subsistence farmer. In the long run this reversal may be seen as economically rational. If people are in fact subsistence nomads, why pretend they are anything else? Alternatively, a caring society might initiate an educational programme to permit those who desired a more lucrative life to find one. In the short run, however, such abrupt change, instead of progress, produces only poverty.

At the time of writing it is impossible for anyone to predict how, when and whether the countries of the Russian Federation will recover. There are indications that could support long-term optimism, there are others which definitely point the other way. Basically, the only way to reverse the increases in poverty and inequality will be to reverse the general economic, political and social dislocation.

In eastern Europe much is happening and it is probable that normal production and growth will be fully recovered, if not surpassed by the end of the first decade of the twenty-first century. In the meantime, in cities such as Bucharest, there is glitter, bustle and there are also many beggars. In these countries it is possible that the increase in poverty and inequality will persist after production and growth have recovered. If so, there is another thing they will also need to learn from capitalism: how to collect taxes and effectively administer a Welfare State.

CHAPTER 7

GLOBAL FINANCE

Has the great 'globalization' of the world financial system damaged the process of poverty reduction? If so, how? By reducing economic growth, increasing inequality, or both?

By 'globalization' people mean that the electronic computer and communications revolutions have created a single world market for money, or more precisely for banking services – the business of lending and borrowing money. The business of banking has been described as the business of moving money from where it is to where it is needed. This business has always been international. Money could be moved between the ancient Greek city states, and in the Middle Ages bankers in city communes in northern Italy financed projects all over Europe, including the wars of the kings of England. What is being said about the international financial world of today is that its fluidity has become much greater and very much faster. Huge funds can be transferred in seconds, extremely complex contracts (called 'derivatives') relating to future interest rates and exchange rates can be valued and traded. In consequence nationless market forces are said to dominate governments. In the early 1970s the combined foreign-currency reserves of all the world's established governments represented about five hours' turnover of the world's total foreign exchange markets. By the end of the century that figure is down to five minutes. There is an argument that these developments have created instability leading in turn to increased risks, higher long-term investment costs and consequently adverse effects on the 'real' (that is, physical) economies of the world, especially those of the Third World. In effect, it is said that the new developments, unless more carefully regulated, will in the long term slow up economic growth.

A Built-in Paradox

But there is a paradox. There are five kinds of financial movement involved. There is private-sector-to-private-sector short-term fixed-interest money, ditto long- and medium-term (bonds); there is international buying and selling of equity shares, and there is what is called 'direct investment' when a company in one country directly finances a business project in another. Finally there are short- and long-term funds lent by private First World banks and others to Third World governments (government-to-government money is called official aid). If all these kinds of movements have become easier, should not investment by the First World in the Third World (which, as we saw in Chapter 5, increased greatly in the final decade) have been encouraged rather than discouraged, and should not economic growth and poverty reduction also thereby be encouraged rather than discouraged?

The answer is, 'Yes and no'. If instability has increased, there is both encouragement and discouragement. It is possible for private long-term lending to and borrowing by the Third World to go through periods when it runs away with itself. In the nineteenth century it was not uncommon for British investors to buy the bonds of South American railway developments. Today they, and all the rest of the First World, habitually buy the bonds of Latin American governments, banks and many other kinds of enterprises. The same is the case, of course, in respect to East Asia. As in the nineteenth century, so in the twentieth, there are failures and defaults. And as in both centuries these things go in waves, upward waves when borrowing becomes imprudently fast, and large panic withdrawals when what seems like a house of cards appears to be collapsing. In fact, the house-of-cards analogy is imperfect. A Third World country may suffer a *financial* collapse (or at least require a major bail-out, called 'refinancing'), but left behind are important and productive physical structures; in the old days railways and other infrastructures; in the twentieth century substantial quantities of industrial and general commercial capital. It is customary, when a crisis occurs, to say that the physical investments must have been unsound, unbalanced or otherwise unproductive.

Whether or not that is the case, the new capital facilities are likely to be rendering sterling service for many decades, if not half centuries, to come. In other words, it is perfectly possible that a crisis of long-term debt may arise without anything having been fundamentally wrong with the physical projects.

Waves of Crisis

Joseph Stiglitz, Chief Economist of the World Bank, in a wide-ranging critique of the existing global financial system has graphically described the waves of financial crisis that have affected all three worlds in the last quarter of the twentieth century ('More Instruments and Broader Goals', 1998). Two particular 'waves' must be noted – one occurring in Latin America and in Africa running from the late '70s into the late '80s and the other occurring in East Asia running from the late '80s into the late '90s. The first, whose adverse effects on growth and poverty reduction has already been noted, was caused by a surge of private-to-government borrowing as the governments struggled to deal with the adverse effects on their overseas payments balances caused by the great world oil-price hikes of 1973 and 1979. (Why this was necessary in the case of oil-rich Mexico remains a mystery.) When it became apparent that the interest and repayments due on many of these loans could not be supported, a semi-panic occurred, which was eventually calmed by various debt re-scheduling plans, put in place because they were as much in the interest of the creditors as the debtors. Nevertheless, the adverse shock to the basic economies of the debtor countries was severe. In the East Asian case, fast growth produced a kind of financial euphoria, gripping both borrowers and lenders, in the course of which short-term loans were used to finance long-term investments. That is a procedure which works so long as things go up and up. If the physical expansion hiccups, a network of debts and credits begins to unravel resulting in a general reduction in the amount of finance available to service the system. The financial crisis leads to economic depression (again a familiar tale in nineteenth-century England after the Industrial Revolution).

None of this is really new: fast economic growth in a market economy is almost inevitably unstable. What was new in the late twentieth century were two major factors – the domestic banking problem and the foreign exchange problem.

The Domestic Banking Problem

The first new factor lies within the Third World: it is a lag between the development of an open and legitimate banking system on the one hand and the growth of the physical economy on the other. During the uprush, much of the required credit creation is provided by informal personal arrangements, many unwritten, many of dubious morality or legality. In all the East Asian countries outside China, ethnic Chinese people are responsible for a disproportionate amount of business activity and economic development. This group, like other family-conscious expatriate ethnic groups in the world, maintains networks of interpersonal and interfamily financial arrangements based essentially on trust rather than legal contract.

There is nothing intrinsically wrong with these financial methods. In the right circumstances they can produce more money and more flexible investment than the conventional methods of the First World banking system. However, they are also prone to unravel in crisis.

The banking crises in the last quarter of the twentieth century have by no means been confined to the Third and Second Worlds. They have also occurred in the United States (the Savings-and-Loan crisis of the second half of the '80s), Spain, Sweden, Norway and Israel. World Bank research (Caprio and Klingebeil in 'Bank Insolvencies', 1996) has shown that in any country a banking crisis is liable to slow down growth. But it is also the case that it was the faster-growing countries that were generally most prone to crises. When the fast pre-crisis growth rates are averaged with the slow post-crisis rates, the average growth performance of crisis countries is actually better than that of non-crisis countries. This is an extremely important finding. It suggests that in the past fast growth rates followed by banking crises and growth slow-downs have been a rather typical experience for countries whose long-run economic prospects are basically good. Clearly, what is needed is to find a way of avoiding the slow-downs.

Caprio and Klingebeil show conclusively the commonest causes of banking failures have been bad management, weak regulation, fraud and politically motivated lending. The moral is fairly obvious. The solutions will be discussed in the Action Programme in Chapter 9.

The Foreign Exchange Problem

The second and crucially important exacerbating factor is systematic foreign-exchange-rate instability. Although orderly adjustment of exchange rates may often facilitate economic development by permitting trade between countries with otherwise disparate economies, it would probably on balance be better for the Social Welfare of the world if there were a single world government and a single world currency. In the meantime we have to live with the situation that exists. In that situation, as soon as, and often before, there are signs of a financial frisson in a Third World country, there is a possibility (not an inevitability) that massive negative speculation against the country's currency will occur. Instead of the initial decline being dampened by reverse flows, it is reinforced by expectations of further decline, causing yet more adverse speculation. As a result the exchange rate falls to a much lower level than the underlying situation justifies, disrupting the domestic economy: soaring import prices disrupt industrial production, generate inflation and create poverty.

At that stage, an international rescue operation, probably organized and partly financed by the International Monetary Fund (IMF), may well be mounted. Unfortunately, the terms and conditions that are typically imposed are not unlikely to slow up economic growth and also directly increase inequality. The IMF has consequently come up against increasing criticism. It has been criticized for creating high interest rates in developing countries and also for over-emphasizing the desirability of very low rates of inflation, criticized because pushing inflation to very low levels appears on the evidence to be more likely to retard rather than support, economic growth, and it has been criticized for treating private banking crises as if they were necessarily caused by errors of government policy. It is also accused of pressing policies on Third World countries which 'are little more than a proxy for Western, and notably American, commercial interests. Having allowed Western banks to get off scot-free in Thailand and Korea, it played hardball in Indonesia, but this had . . . everything to do with America's desire to topple President Suharto.' (Janet Bush, *The Times*, London, August 1998.) A more general criticism is that the internal culture and research resources of the IMF are inappropriate to the present world.

The Action Programme in Chapter 9 will therefore discuss reform of the IMF and other international financial institutions.

CHAPTER 8

THE ENVIRONMENT

The Nature of the Problem

In the Introduction we saw how the twin tasks of eliminating world poverty and reducing world inequality were complicated by the major problem that the human animal faces in its habitat. We have set out the tasks of eliminating absolute poverty by the year 2050 and of progressively reducing international inequality so that by the end of the twenty-first century the average income per head of what is now the Third World will become equal to what will then be the average income per head of what is now the First World. The problem for the environment lies in the ecological implications of world production. By the year 2050 total world economic activity – the production and consumption of all the different kinds of goods and services – will need to have increased fivefold, as compared to the year 2000. By the end of the twenty-first century that number becomes no less than thirtyfold. Does this mean thirty times more consumption of natural resources, thirty times more energy consumption and carbon emissions, thirty times increase in other kinds of environmental pollution, of water consumption – thirty times more global tourism? Contrary to the common pessimistic view, this writer believes that the right answers to these questions are in most cases, 'Not necessarily'.

There is also the question of the capacity of the planet to produce a sufficient increase in the food supply. Citizens of the First World at the end of the twentieth century are mostly eating more food than is good for them. The average citizen of the Third World is adequately but hardly generously nourished; the below-average citizen is not. The governments of the First World spend much time and energy discouraging their domestic agricultural production. In economic terms, there is a world food surplus. The reason why many people nevertheless go to bed hungry at night is the same in all three Worlds; they don't have enough money. In the past, the United States provided official aid to Third World countries in the form of food but the programme was criticized as a 'dumping scheme' for US farm surpluses and also for discouraging domestic production in the recipient countries. For international policy-makers there are times when it seems they cannot win.

The causes of many contradictions in food policy are thus ultimately due to failures of economic growth. If, as individual Third World countries industrialize, they experience geographical barriers to increasing food production to match new demand, they should in principle be able to import food from geographically better-favoured countries, paying with industrial exports. If a country proves unable to pay for needed food imports, it must be because, owing to insufficient economic growth, it is unable to provide the required exports.

As the world population doubles, the need for food will more than double, but probably not by much. Given what has happened in the past, the necessary increases in yields per unit of land seem feasible. The implications for world agricultural output per unit of labour (in contrast to land) are, of course, much more dramatic. In the twenty-first century, this will need to increase by a factor of ten, mostly in the Third World. Again, given what happened in the First World in the past, there is no reason why change on this scale should not happen in the Third World in the future. The food question will be the subject of another book in this series. Supplies of fish, however, present a special problem, and this issue is discussed later in this chapter.

The major problem for agriculture is social rather than physical. Rather than a physical problem of production, it is a social problem of displaced agriculturalists. Ever since the beginning of the agricultural revolution in the First World three hundred years ago, common lands have been enclosed and small farmers displaced, driven, in effect, into industry. Partha Dasgupta has shown that this process is still happening today in the Amazon basin (*Economic Development and Social Capital*, 1997, and 'The Economics of Poverty in Poor Countries', 1998). World food production has increased, but, unless industrialization is sufficiently rapid, which in Brazil, apparently, it is not, the displaced people suffer hardship or worse. World Social Welfare is by no means necessarily increased. In contrast, in western continental Europe, where the agricultural revolution was not finally completed until the end of the twentieth century, the Common Agricultural Policy of the European Union, costly as it was, effectively delayed the process, and in so doing also substantially softened the potentially adverse effects.

Two major general difficulties affect the assessment of environmental dangers. The first is that the effects are very uncertain. The second is that they are what scientists call 'non-linear', meaning that effects do not move in simple proportion to causes. In particular there may be thresholds. A small degree of global warming may have small effect on average daily air temperatures, but may nevertheless severely increase the incidence of storms and droughts in particular parts of the world. The north-western European climate, having become pleasantly mellower, might turn sharply the other way as ice-shelves break away in the Antarctic and as the natural mechanism that produces the Gulf Stream fails. The argument that effects are non-linear is of crucial importance to the hundred and fifty million humans who live in major land areas around the Equator. North-east Brazil and west-central Africa are leading examples.

The uncertainty and 'non-linearity' problem interact to inhibit simple evaluations of costs and benefits. They make a strong recommendation for 'safety first' to the human race: 'When in doubt, don't.' The fear of catastrophic costs gives the 'Green' environmental movement great force.

Unfortunately, the policy of 'safety first' also has a cost. That cost is not, as it is sometimes presented, merely modest reduction in the growth of prosperity among already prosperous people. It is a massive cost to the world's poor. It used to be said that the idea of raising the Third World to the economic level of the First World was ridiculous, simply because, long before that point is reached, the planet's natural resources would be completely exhausted. That isn't true. Indeed, on an extreme view, the exaggerated version of the 'Green' thesis could almost be seen as a conspiracy against the poor. It is not of course what the movement's supporters intend.

There are four main types of environmental problem. There is exhaustion of natural resources, especially fossil fuels. There is pollution of all kinds, of rivers, of lakes, of oceans and of the air we breathe. There is damage to the atmosphere. There is human congestion. Of all of these, at the turn of the twentieth and twenty-first centuries, the danger of global warming through damage to the atmosphere is the greatest cause of concern. Therefore, in this discussion, we come to it last.

The Demand and Supply of Energy

In the mid-1970s, when concern about environmental limits to growth began to engage the attention of the world (in the Club of Rome's *The Limits to Growth*; in Ed Mishan's *The Costs of Growth;* in Fred Hirsch's *The Social Limits to Growth*) the prices of a wide range of basic commodities, such as non-ferrous metals, had experienced a major boom. The price of oil, however, had completely exploded, causing a uniquely severe world inflation. At the end of the '70s the oil price again rose sharply, causing more inflation. Actually, world prices and oil prices were chasing each other so that the 'real' price of oil (the price adjusted for inflation) was never so high as it seemed. And by the end of the century the real price had fallen to significantly *below* the level at which it had stood in the late '60s when the whole saga began.

Anyone who predicted in 1977 that the oil price would be so low in 1997 would have seemed mad. Nevertheless this has happened. There are two reasons. More oil has been found and major technical changes have been stimulated to reduce the amount of energy required to produce an average 'real' (inflation-adjusted) dollar of GDP. Between 1970 and the year 2000 world GDP will have increased by 150 per cent, while world energy consumption will have increased by only 75 per cent. In the future, it is expected that every 10 per cent increase in world GDP will require only a 5 per cent increase in energy.

At first sight, the future of the world energy balance still remains a problem. If one applies the law of five and ten (5 per cent more energy for each 10 per cent of economic growth) to the world economic growth targets set out in the Introduction to this book, one finds that by the year 2050 world energy consumption will nearly double, and that by the end of the century it will have increased, as compared with the year 2000, by a factor of five. Quite apart from the question of global warming, where is all this fuel going to come from?

In fact, despite the new discoveries of oil, it is possible that by the middle of the twenty-first century all the oil and gas fields that we know, plus any that will be discovered in the meantime, will have been exhausted. But there remains a huge reserve of energy in the form of coal. In the second half of the century, in the absence of major new technology, synthetic oil made from coal may become the world's major energy source. Solar energy will also become increasingly 'economic' and is likely to play an additional major role. The conclusion, which will surprise, if not shock, many people, is that the world energy *supply* is not a problem.

The Water Supply

Unlike fossil fuels, water is not an 'exhaustible' resource. When fossil fuels are broken down to create energy they cannot be put together again. That is not the case with water. The total amount on our planet – about fifteen hundred trillion cubic metres – is fixed. Nature recycles it continuously through the familiar chain of evaporation, condensation and precipitation. The human race (and, of course, to a lesser extent, other animals) intercepts the water chain for its own purposes. We currently actually succeed in diverting no more than one part in a million of the total stock.

After using the water for various bodily and industrial purposes we expel it, often in a polluted state. After being expelled from the human cycle the water may undergo various adventures, including temporary residence in underground lakes called aquifers, but always eventually rejoins the basic cycle in a pure form.

The amount of water the human race can divert and use depends on the location of the population and the quantity of man-made water-works. In the past two hundred years, the total amount has increased by many many times. When the population again doubles in the twenty-first century, the further increase in water use will need to be considerably more than double, because with higher GDP per head there is always greater water use per head. When every human being on the planet lives in a home with a water closet, when world production of food has doubled and world total GDP has increased by the amount necessary to meet our objectives, it can be estimated that human water consumption (including drinking, sanitary and all other domestic use, plus industry, commerce and agricultural irrigation) will double between 2000 and 2050, and treble by 2100. Technically and macro-economically this is clearly feasible: even at the end we would only be making use of one part in a quarter million of the planetary water stock. Of course, massive investment is required, but that is the case with all human economic advance. The required investment in sewage works and water supplies would not represent a disproportionate share of the total world investment required for the economic growth required to meet the twin objectives.

As in the case of food, so with water, the real problems, rather than technical, are essentially geographical and social. A disproportionate share of the world's poor people currently live in regions especially vulnerable to 'water stress', in other words regions where the costs of increasing water supplies are especially high. At first sight it seems that to provide the already hard-pressed inhabitants with adequate supplies in the context of economic growth and poverty reduction means moving water or people, or both. In other words, money or social disturbance, or both. Fortunately there are numerous practical ways of promoting sustainable water management by education and investment at the local level, and the international development community is actively encouraging these, both by research and by official aid tied to health and water projects (*Water Matters*, Department for International Development, 1997; *Strategic Approaches to Freshwater Management*, United Nations, 1998).

The Problem of General Pollution

The most significant type of general pollution is that caused by the exhausts of internal combustion engines powered by fossil fuel. No one really knows how bad this would be if every petrol (gasoline) engine had an efficient catalytic converter and every diesel engine were always tuned and run in such a way that combustion was always complete: at the present time even a perfectly run diesel engine emits invisible particles which are seriously damaging to health.

The programme for reducing world general inequality implies that the average person in the Third World will in due course have all the capabilities of the average person in the First World. A fundamental modern capability is personal freedom to travel, either by means of a personal vehicle or by effective and genuinely convenient public transport. In the First World there may well be an increasingly wide move to restrain the use of personal vehicles and to improve public transport. In addition, it is certain that before the middle of the century, totally non-polluting cars will be available and will be the only kind allowed. In that case, it is perfectly possible that the number of personal vehicles in the world will increase by a much larger factor than the increase in world population. In fact, if general world inequality is to be reduced, that is inevitable.

A hugely larger area of the planet's surface will be urbanized (but food production will be sustained), and inside these areas and between them there will be billions of personal vehicles. Given clean technology, this will not be a nightmare of pollution, but of congestion.

There are of course many other forms of pollution, of oceans, lakes and rivers, and by garbage, and so forth. They are again essentially problems of social and economic organization. The things that are polluted are those things that either no one privately owns or no government effectively regulates. In First World countries, most of the time, urban garbage is effectively collected and, increasingly, separated and recycled. In the Third World countries, despite the cheapness of the type of labour needed to do the work, that is widely not the case. The difference is money. More precisely, public money. The local governments apparently do not have the tax revenue to pay garbage collectors. Alternatively, they lack the necessary political will. The streets of London, for example, have much improved in recent years, but the real cost of garbage collection has actually been reduced.

The change was simply due to better organization and increased efficiency.

Destruction of forests, either by felling or fire, is a form of pollution. It is very simple to stop. Pass a law and enforce it. If First World governments can do this, so can Third World governments. Poverty is no excuse. On the contrary, the poorer the country, the higher the priority for protecting its resources. The poor always suffer more from pollution than the rich.

The Fish Supply

Overfishing is a classic example of the inability of the free-market system to cope with certain types of problems. The ocean is owned by no one, so fishermen and their customers do not have to pay to use it. As the intensity of fishing of a species is increased, a threshold may be passed whereby the species may be forced into temporary or permanent extinction. The potential cost of taking one more fish is therefore much greater than the actual cost of catching it. A free market, however, has no way of compelling the consumer to face this cost. Were that not the case, the price of the species would rise sufficiently to discourage consumption sufficiently to forestall the disaster. Only government regulation can solve the problem. Since the oceans are not owned by nations, international cooperation is required, which is always difficult. For some reason, government representatives always seem more concerned for the short term interests of their producers (such as fishermen) than the long term interests of their consumers.

As most readers know, some effective international collective action (for example in the case of whales and drift-net fishing) does occur, but the results are imperfect. What happens if that continues? Suppose that, as a result of the growth of GDP the world demand for fish multiplies by a factor of, say, five, while international regulation still does not improve? There would be some increase in consumption from the huge stocks of fish that exist in the world's oceans that are currently unfished because the species are unfamiliar. There would also be a considerable increase in fish farming. Finally, if these two sources of replacement were inadequate to fill the gap between demand and supply, the price of fish would rise and the world's consumers would seek alternative sources of protein.

It would be much better to handle the problem by international co-operation and management, but if the human race remains so feckless that this does not happen, the end result will not be fatal. If in the course of eliminating world poverty, we all have to eat proportionately less fish than would otherwise have been the case, it would be sad (and not healthy), but it would not be fatal.

The Problem of Congestion

Despite the fact that it is daily in the minds of most First World citizens, traffic congestion is not really the most serious example of the general problem of human congestion of the planet. It is basically a problem of social organization: too many people, in their cars, wanting to be in the same place at the same time. It has a tendency to resolve itself, either by road construction, reconstruction or, in the absence of either, by the simple fact that when it becomes bad enough, people travel elsewhere or less. Nobody denies that traffic congestion in towns is a problem. Quite probably we shall increasingly take the rational step of either prohibiting or charging for entry of lightly laden private cars into towns.

The real problem of human congestion is more general. It was first identified in a brilliant book entitled *The Social Limits to Growth* (1977) by the economist Fred Hirsch, who died cruelly young shortly after writing it. His thesis was not initially directed to the problem of poverty, but to that of affluence. He argued that as consumers became richer they naturally desired to devote an increasing proportion of their total resources on leisure activities whose supplies were inherently limited and inherently prone to congestion and pollution. For example, while Hirsch was writing the book he told the author that he believed that before long the British government would have to pass regulations restraining individuals from acquiring 'second homes' in the countryside. As more and more people wanted to visit the countryside, or ancient cities and monuments or clean sunny beaches, by congesting these facilities, they would destroy their value. Hence,

Hirsch argued, in the end there is a basic upper limit to the material ascent of the human race.

Some people, including the present writer, are not convinced of the practical weight of the Hirsch thesis in relation to affluent peoples, but can see nevertheless that it is very relevant to the problem of global inequality. At the present time, people with average incomes in the First World mostly have enough money to engage to a certain degree, if they wish, in global tourism. There are many millions of global tourists and as First World average income continues to rise, there will be many more. But that is nothing compared to the implications of a thirtyfold rise in world GDP. Working hours will fall and there will be potentially a vast increase in the demand for leisure activities. Will the Hirsch theorem, applied on a global scale, then put an absolute block on the process? Will all the beaches and other desirable areas, throughout the world, become hopelessly congested?

It is this writer's pure hunch that the answer is again negative. He suspects that innovation on the one hand and the opening up of as yet untouched resources on the other, will in fact, as in the case of all the other environmental problems already discussed, resolve the dilemma.

Global Warming

Although there are some competent people who claim that the threat of global warming is based on no solid evidence (in fact some of these people are effectively saying that the scare is virtually a scientific red herring), the current weight of both evidence and opinion goes firmly the other way. When organic fossil fuels (whose chemical structure is based on rings of carbon atoms) are burned for energy they are broken down into basic carbon. In the ordinary course of events the resulting carbon particles are then released into the atmosphere. There, as a consequence of the action of the sun's rays they combine with oxygen to form carbon dioxide gas. Like the glass roof of a greenhouse, this gas has the property of letting through the heat of the sun but not hot air coming in the opposite direction – hence the term 'greenhouse effect'.

Ever since the first industrial revolution the citizens of the First World have been emitting increasing amounts of carbon, and the cumulative amount is now one-twentieth of one per cent of all the air and other gases in the atmosphere, as compared with one-thirtieth of one per cent when the process started. According to an intergovernmental group of experts, if emissions continued to rise according to the historic trend, by the year 2050 the level of atmospheric carbon dioxide, as compared with the pre-industrial level, would have doubled. The average climate temperature would then rise by several degrees, enough to cause a one-metre (three-foot) rise in the sea level and adverse effects on agriculture in most regions near the equator. Other regions (such as Russia), however, would benefit and the net effect on world food supply is uncertain: estimates vary from bad to slightly beneficial.

Agriculture, however, is not the only source of potential cost (or benefit). Other costs include those of protecting coasts from the rising waters (or of providing new homes for the fifty million or so people worldwide who would otherwise be displaced); of resolving the situation of the inhabitants of low-lying islands (fortunately not much more than a quarter of one per cent of the world's population); of the effects of loss of river flow (causing increased costs of mitigating pollution); of the effects of increased incidence of hurricanes, floods and heatwaves. The monetary equivalent of all these costs has been estimated by experts (for the year 2050) at $1^1/_3$ per cent of total annual GDP for the First World and $1^2/_3$ per cent of GDP for the Third World, averaging just under $1^1/_2$ per cent of GDP for the whole world (*Economic and Social Dimensions of Climate Change*, Inter-governmental Panel, 1996).

Bearing in mind that the world's GDP normally grows by 3 per cent, one result of these calculations is to ask what all the fuss is about. There are three crucial answers. The first is that they do not take account of the implications of a programme, such as suggested in this book, for reducing world inequality. The second is that they do not take full account of possible 'non-linear' catastrophes, which, if they occur, are much more serious for poor countries than for rich countries. The third is that they do not, as such, project beyond 2050. Yet, as the experts recognize, if nothing is done, the carbon-dioxide concentration and temperature will rise, and will go on increasing until, at the end of the twenty-second century, the temperature reaches Jurassic levels and the human situation becomes intolerable.

It follows that what is needed is a programme that will stabilize the rise in carbon dioxide at one-fifteenth of one per cent of the total atmosphere – twice the level that existed before industrialization began. This means, in fact, that annual carbon emissions must also not rise above twice their levels in 2000. Given that our programme for the elimination of poverty and inequality requires a doubling of world energy consumption by 2050 and, as compared with the year 2000, a fivefold rise by the year 2100, how could that possibly be done?

The answer is, firstly, technology that will drastically reduce the amount of carbon sent out into the air for every unit of carbon-fuel consumed and, secondly, a major reduction in the proportion of the world's energy that is supplied by carbon fuels as against other sources, such as solar energy and water power. But these changes may be quite expensive. Because no person or institution has to pay when she, he or they put carbon into the atmosphere, the market system will not therefore induce the necessary changes to happen. An effective intergovernmental action programme is therefore absolutely essential, and will be part of the subject of our final chapter.

A Provisional Conclusion

Many things need to be done to mitigate environmental problems. In the ordinary course of events some will get done and some will not. That is the way of the world. When failures occur the results will generally be adaptation rather than catastrophe. The fact that as a species some of us are already planning as much as a century ahead in the hope of forestalling catastrophe attests yet again to our remarkable mental and social capacities.

In the case of global warming, however, an effective intergovernmental action programme is essential. Without it we fail not only the poor, but our species and our planet. A practical programme, that would have no adverse effects on the programme for the Third World to catch up the First World, is described in the next chapter.

CHAPTER 9

THE ACTION PROGRAMME

'Our future is not inevitable. We can affect its course if we know where we might want to go.'

Yorick Blumenfeld, *Towards the Millennium*, 1997

'Few – if any – of the grandiose claims for the post-Keynesian era [after 1973] have been realised. Growth has not been faster; it has been slower. Unemployment is not lower, but higher; political life was not cleansed, but became a cesspit. Optimists would say that everything will eventually turn out for the best, pessimists would argue that the current rippling financial crisis cannot be dismissed simply as a blip.'

Larry Elliot, *Guardian*, 25 August 1998

The Background

This book has argued that whether or not the setbacks in the Second and Third Worlds that began in late 1997, represented blip or something more serious, there are no technical, economic or insurmountable environmental reasons why the benefits of the great economic ascent of the human race, which began in northern Europe 250 years ago, and is still largely confined to the First World, should not be shared by the rest of the world. The real obstacles are social, political and cultural. The global destiny of the human race lies in our hands. The situation at the end of the twentieth century is not only intolerable but also unnecessary. Consequently, we have suggested that:

1 It is economically and technically possible to greatly reduce absolute poverty in the Third World by the year 2015, and to eliminate absolute poverty in the Third World by the year 2050.

2 It is possible to equalize the average standard of living in the Third and First Worlds by the end of the twenty-first century, and to make substantial progress towards that goal by 2050.

3 World population growth will naturally cease at a manageable level but will nevertheless create major costs. On present trends, stability will occur at a world population around ten millions, or double the level at the end of the twentieth century. Stability at a lower level is possible and would be desirable. The higher the level to which the world population rises before it stabilizes, the less easy it will be to eliminate poverty. Every effort needs to be made, therefore, to encourage the declining trend of fertility.

4 The fundamental engine of poverty reduction in the Third World is long-term growth of *average* income per head. The alternative of trying to achieve the objectives by cash transfers from rich to poor, either within the Third World or between the First and Third Worlds, is not feasible. For example, if, in deference to environmental arguments, the average income per head of the whole world were frozen at the year 2000 level, and then redistributed so that income per head in the two worlds was equalized, the standard of living of the First World would have to be reduced by more than 75 per cent: in return, the Third World would gain less than 20 per cent. Since the citizens of the First World are never going to agree to that, if one holds the view that the planet's economic activity should be frozen, one must also be implicitly advocating virtually freezing the level of poverty and inequality.

5 Propositions 1, 2, 3 and 4 together imply that world economic production would multiply by a factor of five by the middle of the twenty-first century and by a factor of thirty by the century's end. (For environmental implications, see 12 below.)

6 The key factors leading Third World countries to take off into rapid growth are culture, education and good government.

7 In the First World, there remains, however, a potential problem that the new technology may create permanent forces tending to increase inequality, in the sense of increasing the comparative economic handicap of people born with interacting social, ability and educational disadvantages. If that is the case, both economic and moral arguments state that there should be an increase in the redistributive element in taxation.

8 Development aid has a major role to play in supporting and supplementing the process of economic growth.

9 The new poverty in the First World is mainly the result of unemployment, which is in turn mainly the result of macro-economic problems. These are that total production has not grown at the rate necessary to take up the slack in the labour market; the burden has fallen hardest on the least skilled workers. If the macro-economy is managed properly, many of the forces causing the New Poverty will wither. Good macro-economic management means maintaining low real-interest rates and, while avoiding fast or accelerating inflation, also avoiding excessive caution and dysfunctional inflation targets.

10 The process of 'transition' in the ex-Communist countries caused massive increases in poverty and inequality mainly as a result of heavy absolute declines in total GDP, plus the effects of the breakdown of government and disorderly privatization. These symptoms are at their worst in Russia and the Ukraine. There is at present no obvious solution to this very grave problem.

11 The 'globalization' of the world financial system, which should have facilitated the flow of capital into the Third World has had dysfunctional features that can have the opposite effect. We discuss some solutions on pp. 111–113 below.

12 The problems of the planet's environment need not block the programme of poverty reduction. Many are issues of social, political

and economic organization that can be managed by good government or alternatively will resolve themselves imperfectly but not catastrophically. The problem of global warming is a major exception, since the programme to eliminate international inequality will require a large further increase in world energy consumption. The necessary supplies of energy can be found, but their consumption has to be achieved alongside a massive reduction in the amount of carbon emitted per unit of energy created. This will require particularly strong intergovernmental action.

General Policies

Some of the things that need to happen are already beginning to happen. Others are matters of general policy and attitude. One cannot wake up in the morning and command all governments to be good and all reactionary cultures to change. One can, however, do many things on a wide front on a pragmatic basis to encourage desirable change and to give practical and moral support to all who are trying to achieve it.

One major desirable development is that policy-makers throughout the world should become less timorous of 'interfering' in the social affairs of so-called nation states. Most nations are at least two nations, rich and poor. The poor are not represented at the international negotiating table. A 'national' government has no moral right to pristine independence if that independence, for example, means that primary education for the benefit of the poor is neglected. Any person who cares seriously about the world's poor must think seriously about the concept of nationhood.

Some Key Regions

CHINA It is not easy for individuals or governments outside China to feel that they have the capacity to influence the course of economic events in that great country. At the end of the twentieth century the government is courageously attempting to sustain economic growth by reforming and partly privatizing state industries. In the process they have encountered the same bind that has created the new poor in the First World. As workers are displaced, the total economy must grow fast enough to re-employ them; otherwise they will not be re-employed. There are reports of increasing unemployment and political unrest. The outside world is likely to see these developments as linked to the question of the development of civil rights and civil liberties.

Outsiders need to be sympathetic to China's problems. The world owes a considerable debt to the Chinese leaders for three things: for showing that Third World countries can take off; for sparing us the nightmare that has become Russia and the Ukraine; and for making a vital contribution to world population control, albeit by brutal methods.

INDIA The 'traditionalist' regions of India, containing a substantial proportion of all the poor people in the world, are a major problem. The country has maintained elective democracy but unfortunately at a cost in some regions of grave developmental conservatism. The price is paid by the poor. In that context the current national political situation is not a happy one. The international community should take all possible general and specific steps to encourage people in India who strive for a different direction. India never receives as much attention from the development community as her large population warrants. In particular, India receives a ridiculously small amount of official development aid. She should receive more aid (see below) specifically targeted at primary education, sewage works and water supply.

India's leaders should also ask themselves the question of why the country, whose textile industry in the seventeenth century was the strongest in the world, and whose people today show exceptional ability in that field, today has total exports, per head of population, at less than a quarter of the level of other large countries in the Third World, such as China and Indonesia.

BRAZIL Despite the fact that in the late '70s Brazil showed many signs of impending take-off, with brisk growth of manufacturing exports, the country still has the worst income distribution in the world and a controversial environmental record. The result is burning forests and fifty million poor. Both the nation's leaders and the international community need to consider Brazil's problems more seriously.

SUB-SAHARAN AFRICA Because it is divided into a number of relatively small countries this region receives a disproportionate amount of official aid. It is also, as is well known, extremely poor. On present trends the region will be the last in the world to achieve population stability, and when it does it will hold a much larger share of total world population than in the year 2000. Inevitably, the region is in danger of containing an increasing share of the world's absolute poor. Apart from good government, the most important priority is population control.

The quality of government is improving and official aid donors are explicitly encouraging this. The general direction of international policy towards the region is on the right lines.

The First World

In the Anglo-Saxon countries the governments are attempting to remedy the 'welfare dependency' aftermath of fifteen years of massive unemployment by a variety of direct actions such as the British 'welfare to work'. Partly by luck and partly by good guidance, although they do not like to use the term, they have nearly reached 'full employment'. In both countries the continuing debate on macro-economic management revolves around the balance between avoiding unemployment and the control of inflation. Unemployment at the end of the 1990s is nearly down to its pre-disaster levels. If such a favourable balance can be maintained, the new poverty will probably be eliminated within a decade: already by 1997 there were statistical signs of improvement in the relative position of the lowest-paid workers. Alternatively, if high unemployment returns, no amount of direct action will prevent poverty returning.

In continental Europe, about to enter its currency union, double-digit unemployment persists, and there is a widespread defeatist attitude. Particularly in France, people seem to think there is a fixed amount of work to be done, which had best be shared out in various ways. One way is keeping young people out of the workforce: the unemployment rate among French people aged 25–30 runs at an incredible 25 per cent, while that among older people is less than half. Another method is compulsory reduction of working hours. The fallacy behind the whole situation is an implicit belief that the rate of growth of GDP, and hence also the amount of work available, is immutable.

The capability deprivation implied by European youth unemployment does not, as we have seen, involve a large amount of income poverty; instead, people speak of 'social exclusion'. In fact France, which at one time had a high level of general inequality, has in the past twenty years reduced inequality to nearer the world average. But the unemployment situation in France is producing increasingly disturbing political symptoms.

A major controversy exists as to whether not only in France but also in Germany a range of institutions in the labour market, which tend to restrain inequality and poverty, nevertheless discourage economic growth by making labour 'too expensive'. In particular, attention focuses on legal barriers to dismissing workers, which in turn discourage employers from recruitment. It is a difficult debate to resolve, but undoubtedly there is a vital need for a massive change in policy- making priorities.

Specific Actions

OFFICIAL AID   The world level is ridiculously low and should be doubled or trebled. Unfortunately, at the present time most First World Governments are mainly concerned with restraining, rather than expanding public expenditure. One cause is the Welfare State cost of the unemployment disaster in the First World and its aftermath. Better management of First World economies could lead to an eventual increase in aid. Targeted aid should be diverted to large countries.

PRIMARY EDUCATION   Discussions should be held between the OECD Development Assistance Committee, the World Bank and the United Nations Development Programme with a view to planning and implementing a World Primary Education Programme. This would select target countries and sub-regions where adult illiteracy is high for programmes of specific reductions, based on moderate injections of outside money tied to major improvements in administration and attitude. The targets in these programmes should relate not to money spent but to numbers of children actually educated to certain levels, and also to the sustained maintenance of these levels.

SAFE WATER We saw that a plan to eliminate unsafe water supply throughout the world inside a couple of decades could be financed by a tax of only one or two cents in the dollar on every First World income in the top 20 per cent of wealth (p. 64). Since this, sadly, is unlikely to happen through government action, a world-wide voluntary charitable fund should be created to attempt carry out the same programme. If only one in five people in the First World richest 20 per cent contributed, they would need to covenant five cents in a dollar of income over their lifetimes. If rich people in the Third World also contributed, the burden would be so much the less.

THE INTERNATIONAL FINANCIAL SYSTEM The instability of the system (see Chapter 7) is a serious threat to our problem of world poverty elimination and international inequality reduction. It is a threat because it threatens economic growth. One problem is exchange-rate instability, another is banking instability.

In connection with exchange-rate instability, the most powerful proposal is the 'Tobin Tax' proposed by economics Nobel Laureate James Tobin, as described in *Reflections on Human Development* (1996), edited by the late and greatly lamented economist Mabub al-Haq. It is in effect a turnover tax on all international transactions. Set at a low level it will not significantly restrict genuine long-term financial investments, but will act as a severe brake on speculators who move into and out of given currencies many times a day. The Tobin Tax will not however prevent catastrophic currency collapse, out of all proportion to underlying real causes, such as occurred in 1997–98 in the cases of Thailand, South Korea, Malaysia and the Philippines.

Banks require regulation and supervision because when one bank fails, other banks and indeed the whole national economy can be severely damaged by the knock-on effect. When this happens the supply of money and credit contracts, as does the real economy. This has been reasonably effectively recognized in western Europe and north America since the middle of the nineteenth century. In the rest of the world, including Japan, it is also recognized, but perhaps less effectively. Mr Nick Leeson, operating from Singapore, brought down an old-established British bank (Barings, so long-established that it was involved in banking crises in the nineteenth century) by actions which were mostly not illegal in Singapore. Finally in the last hour, Leeson committed a single act of forgery which, though a criminal offence in Singapore, might not have proved an extraditable offence in London, and thus ended up in a Singapore jail. His dramatic story is a perfect illustration of the need for worldwide banking regulation. Barings' international activities were not being externally supervised because they did not come within the scope of any national jurisdiction. Nor were they being internationally supervised because no effective international supervision system exists. Finally Leeson's Singapore operations were not effectively internally supervised because the London management, influenced, according to Leeson's account (*Rogue Trader*, 1996), by the massive profits and bonuses he was supposedly earning for them, turned several blind eyes to his obviously reckless operations.

It is now essential to move forward from national regulation and supervision to some form of global equivalent, in effect a World Financial Authority, such as was recently suggested by the influential British economist, John Eatwell (*International Capital Markets and the Future of Economic Policy*, 1998). In the absence of a new international regime (the existing powers of the Bank for International Settlements in Basle are too weak), crashes and crises will inevitably recur. Why? Because there is too much money to be made in the upswing. Although the Barings' crash of 1995 did not provoke an immediate general crisis, it was a forerunner of the general international financial crisis which came a few years later.

The other vital task is to undertake a range of reforms and developments designed to minimize the occurrence of both currency and banking crises. The International Monetary Fund was created to help stabilize exchange rates, but has no expertise relating to banking stability in the private sector, and has also proved to be out of its depth in understanding the general nature of the international financial problems of the late 1990s. The IMF needs to be reformed or replaced.

All regulation has costs but the benefits of greater international banking regulation, especially for the world's poor, would far outweigh the costs. Governments have much more power over markets than they suppose. The markets need governments, if only to help collect their debts. The governments need markets to collaborate in the international process to eliminate poverty.

Global Warming

There has to be a heavy reduction in the amount of carbon emitted per unit of energy produced. The major source is the emissions of electric-power stations. The technology has to be changed to 'scrub out' and dispose of the carbon. The technology exists, or can be developed, but it will cost money. At the Tokyo intergovernmental conference on global warming of 1997, quite complicated schemes of targets and quotas were negotiated in which the situation of the Third World was politically delicate. Third World countries currently emit much less carbon, *per head*, than First World countries, but because of the difference in total populations, the total global emissions of the Third World are equal to those of the First World. In addition, pre-industrial countries will suffer more severe costs from global warming than will post-industrial countries. Nevertheless, it is not reasonable to expect poor countries to submit to severe anti-emission costs while they are still poor.

Dr Jae Edmonds, of the Pacific North West National Laboratory, Washington DC, has published a paper (in *Energy and Environment*, May 1998) outlining a rather simple plan which would help resolve this problem. In the First World, all new fossil-fuel power stations must be completely clean after the year 2020. And after that year, all

First World synthetic oil production (from coal, for example) must use a completely clean conversion process, and after the year 2050 all new oil-refineries must eliminate carbon from their products and international trade in refined products must be wound down. No Third World country would be required to conform to these rules until it reached an income per head, adjusted for international price levels, of half the average of the First World. In other words, poor countries would join the club if and when they had taken off into fast growth.

If the foregoing plan is fed into a computer, on the assumption that countries take off one after another through the first seventy-five years of the twenty-first century, leading to an eventual result consistent with our economic-growth targets, total carbon dioxide in the atmospheres would stabilize at the desired level, namely twice the level of the early nineteenth century. There will be moderate warming, the main costs of which, as already mentioned will fall on pre-industrial countries.

This conclusion leads to the conclusion of our book. As Dr Edmonds has pointed out, a country which is today pre-industrial and poor has everything to gain from achieving economic take-off as soon as possible. By that means, not only does it raise the total economic welfare (Social Welfare) of its own citizens through all future time, but also minimizes the likely costs to themselves of the moderate warming which, subject to good management, will be the necessary accompaniment of the great twenty-first century prospective break-through in human economic happiness to which this book has aspired.

This leads to the ultimate moral for the whole development community and therefore to our conclusion. For the First World, maintain good macro-economic management. For the Third World, industrialization, as rapidly as possible. We took millions of years to evolve biologically to where we are today. Only ten thousand years ago, with the discovery of agriculture, we initiated the cultural (in contrast to biological) development that enabled us to transcend our physical environment. It was only three hundred years ago that the First World discovered mechanization, industrialization and economic growth. Surely those last discoveries can be spread to the rest of the world inside another century?

Bibliography

GENERAL

Barclay, P. ed., *Inquiry into Income and Wealth*, vol. 1, Joseph Rowntree Foundation, York, 1995

Blumenfeld, Y., *Towards the Millenium: Optimistic Visions for Change*, London, 1998

Caprio, G., and D. Klingebiel, 'Bank Insolvencies: Cross Country Experience', *World Bank Policy Research Working Paper, 1620*, Washington, DC, 1996

Carlen, C., *The Papal Encyclicals, 1903 1939*, Raleigh, VA, 1981

Dasgupta, P., *Economic Development and Social Capital*, Cambridge, 1997

—, 'The Economics of Poverty in Poor Countries', *Scandinavian Journal of Economics*, vol. 100, no. 1, pp. 41–68, 1998

Davies, N., *The Dark Heart: the Shocking Truth about Hidden Britain*, London, 1998

Disraeli, B., *The Two Nations, 1861*, republished Oxford, 1980

Eatwell, J., *International Capital Markets and the Future of Economic Policy*, Institute of Public Policy Research, London, 1998

Edmonds, J., and M. Wise, 'Building Backstop Technologies to Implement the Framework Convention on Climate Change', *Energy & Environment*, May, 1998

al-Haq, M., I. Kaul and I. Grunberg, eds, *The Tobin Tax: Coping with Financial Volatility*, Oxford, 1996

Harsanyi, J., *Essays on Ethics, Social Behaviour and Scientific Explanation*, Dordrecht, 1976

Hirsch, F., *The Social Limits to Growth*, London, 1977

Leeson, N., *Rogue Trader*, London, 1996

Lundquist, J., and P. Gleick, *The World's Water Resources in the 21st Century*, Stockholm Environment Institute, 1997

Maddison, A., *Dynamic Forces in Economic Development*, Oxford, 1991

—, *Explaining the Performance of Nations*, Aldershot, and Brookfield, VT, 1995

—, *Monitoring the World Economy, 1820–1992*, Paris, OECD Development Centre, 1995

Marks, H., *Mr Nice*, London, 1997

Marris, R., *How to Save the Underclass*, London, 1996

Mishan, E., *The Costs of Economic Growth*, London, 1969

Moss, B. and J. Michie, *The Single Currency in National Perspective: A Community in Crisis?*, London, 1998

Ng, Y.-K., 'Utilitarianism: a Defence' and 'Pure Egalitarianism: a Critique', 1997, papers obtainable from the Department of Economics, Monash University, Australia 3168

Patel, I., *Equity in a Global Society*, Centenary Lecture, London School of Economics, London, 1995

Pullan, B., *Rich and Poor in Renaissance Venice*, Oxford, 1971

Rawls, J., *A Theory of Justice*, Cambridge, Mass., 1971

Sen, A., *On Economic Inequality*, Oxford, 1997

Stiglitz, J., 'More Instruments and Broader Goals: Moving towards a Post-Washington Consensus', *WIDER Annual Lectures 2*, Helsinki, UNU/WIDER, 1998

Young, M., *The Rise of the Meritocracy*, London, 1958

OFFICIAL REPORTS

Economic and Social Dimensions of Climate Change, Intergovernmental Panel on Climate Change, Cambridge, 1996

Eliminating World Poverty: a Challenge for the 21st Century, White Paper on International Development, British Government, Cmd 3789, 1997

Gallup Political and Economic Index, London, 1995

Growth and Poverty in Developing Countries, The World Bank Staff Working Paper No. 309, Washington, DC, 1979

Human Development Report 1997, for United Nations, Oxford, 1997

Poverty in the Transition Economies, United Nations Regional Bureau for Europe and UNDP, New York, 1998

Strategic Approaches to Freshwater Management, Report of the Secretary General, United Nations (E/CN.17/1998/2), New York, 1998

Trade and Development Report, United Nations Conference on Trade and Development, Geneva, 1997

Water Matters, Department for International Development, London, 1997

ECONOMIC GROWTH

Agarwala, A., and S. Singh, eds, *The Economics of Underdevelopment*, Oxford, 1958

Allen, T., and A. Thomas, eds, *Poverty and Development in the 1990s*, Oxford, 1992

Arestis, P., and P. Demetriades, 'Financial Development and Economic Growth', *Economic Journal*, vol. 107, No. 442, pp. 783–800, May 1997

Bauer, P.T., *The Development Frontier*, London, 1991

Cassen, R, *Does Aid Work?*, Oxford, 1986

Chambers, R., *Rural Development*, London, 1983

Clegg, S., and G. Redding, eds, *Capitalism in Contrasting Cultures*, Berlin, 1990

Colclough, C., and J. Manor, eds, *States or Markets?*, Oxford, 1991

Cornia, A. G., R. Jolly and F. Stewart, eds, *Adjustment with a Human Face*, Oxford, 1987

Dasgupta, P., and K.G. Mäler, eds, *The Environment and Emerging Development Issues*, for United Nations University World Institute for Development Economics Research, Helsinki and Oxford, 1997

Drèze, J., and A. Sen, eds, *The Political Economy of Hunger*, Oxford, 1990

Griffin, K., *Alternative Strategies for Economic Development*, London, 1989

—, and John Knight, *Human Development and the International Development Strategy for the 1990s*, London, 1990

al-Haq, M., *Reflections on Human Development*, Oxford, 1995

Higgins, B., *Economic Development: Principles, Problems and Policies*, London, 1959

Hirsch, F., *The Social Limits to Growth*, London, 1977

Hirschman, A., *The Strategy of Economic Development*, New Haven, NJ, 1980

Hollis, C., *Redistribution with Growth: Policies to Improve Income Distribution in Developing Countries in the Context of Economic Growth*, Oxford, 1974

Landes, D.S., *The Wealth and Poverty of Nations*, London, 1998

Lewis, W. A., *Education and Economic Development*, Saskatchewan, 1965

—, *The Theory of Economic Growth*, London, 1955

Martin, K., ed.,*Strategies of Economic Development*, London, 1991

Meadows, D., ed., *The Limits to Growth: Report for the Club of Rome*, New York, 1972

Meier, G., *Leading Issues in Economic Development*, Oxford, 1995

—, and D. Seers, eds, *Pioneers in Development*, for the World Bank, Oxford, 1984 and 1987

Mishan, E., *The Costs of Economic Growth*, London, 1969

Rostow, W.W., *The Process of Economic Growth*, Oxford, 1953

—, *The Stages of Economic Growth: A Non-Communist Manifesto*, Cambridge, 1960

—, (ed.), *The Economics of Take-off into Sustained Growth*: proceedings of conference held by the International Economic Association, London, 1963

—, *Why the Poor Get Richer and the Rich Slow Down*, Austin, TX, 1980

Savoie, D. J. and I. Brecher, eds, *Equity and Efficiency in Economic Development: Essays in Honour of Benjamin Higgins*, Montreal, 1992

Sklair, L., ed.,*Capitalism and Development*, London, 1994

Tawney, R.H., *Religion and the Rise of Capitalism*, London, 1926

Triantis, S., 'Changes in Income, Behaviour and Tastes. Desirable and Feasible Rates of the Economic Development', *South African Journal of Economics*, vol. 63, 1995, pp. 459–72

Weber, M., *The Protestant Ethic and the Spirit of Capitalism*, London, 1930

Wuyts, M., M. Mackintosh and T. Hewitt, eds, *Development Policy and Public Action*, Oxford, 1992

Africa

Cornia, A.G., R. van der Hoeven and T. Mkandawire, eds, *Africa's Recovery in the 1990s*, New York, 1992

Lewis, W. A., *Reflections on Nigeria's Economic Growth*, Paris, OECD, 1967

Sender, J., *Poverty, Class, and Gender in Rural Africa*, London, 1990

East Asia

Higgins, B., *Entrepreneurship and Labor Skills in Indonesian Economic Development: A Symposium*, New York, 1961

Lin, Y., C. Fang and L. Zhou *The China Miracle*, Hong Kong Center for International Research and International Center for Economic Growth (San Francisco), Hong Kong, 1996

Odagiri, H., *Growth through Competition and Competition through Growth: Strategic Management and the Economy in Japan*, Oxford, 1992

Vogel, E. F. *The Four Little Dragons:*
The Spread of Industrialization in East
Asia, Cambridge, Mass., 1991
South Asia
Breman, J., and S. Mundle, eds, *Rural*
Transformation in Asia, Oxford, 1991
Chambers, R., *Poverty in India*,
Brighton, 1988
Drèze, J., and A. Sen, eds, *Indian Development*,
Oxford, 1997
Latin America
Cardoso, F. H., *Dependency and Development*
in Latin America, Berkeley, 1979
Hirschman, A., *A Bias for Hope: Essays*
on Development in Latin America,
New Haven and London, 1971

THE NEW POOR IN THE FIRST WORLD
Atkinson, A., *Incomes and the Welfare State*,
Cambridge, 1995
Barclay, P., ed., *Inquiry into Income*
and Wealth, vol. 1, Joseph Rowntree
Foundation, York, 1995
Burtless, G., R. Freeman and R. Solow,
in J. Norwood, ed., *Widening Earnings*
Inequality, Washington, DC, 1994
Danziger, S., *America Unequal*,
Cambridge, MA, 1995
—, and P. Gottschalk, eds, *Uneven Tides: Rising*
Inequality in America, New York, 1993
Gottschalk, P., 'Changes in the inequality of
family income in seven industrialised
countries', *American Economic Review*, 85,
(AEA Proceedings), pp. 137–141,
May, 1995
al-Haq, M., I. Kaul and I. Grunberg, eds,
The Tobin Tax, Oxford, 1996

Hernstein, R., and C. Murray, *The Bell Curve*,
New York, 1994
Hills, J., *Inquiry into Income and Wealth*,
vol. 2, Joseph Rowntree Foundation,
York, 1995
Hutton, W., *The State We're In*, London,
1995
Machin, S., 'Wage Inequality in the UK',
Policy Studies, Spring, 1996
Mishel, L., and J. Bernstein, *The State of*
Working America, New York, 1994
Nickell, S., and B. Bell, 'The collapse in
demand for the unskilled', *Oxford Review*
of Economic Policy, vol. 11, no. 1,
pp. 40–62, 1995
Wood, A., 'How Trade Hurt Unskilled
Workers', *Journal of Economic*
Perspectives, 9, Summer 1995

WEBSITES
UNCTAD (United Nations Permanent
Conference on Trade and Development)
Studies on East Asian Development;
e-mail: nicole.winch@unctad.org
University of Pennsylvania, via British
Economic and Social Research Council
(ESRC); Penn World Tables on country
populations and purchasing-power-
parity GDPs:
'Penn' at http://sosig.esrc.bris.ac.uk/
World Bank, general publications on poverty
and development:
http://www.worldbank.org
World Bank, Deininger and Squire data set on
inequality within countries:
http://www.worldbank.org/html/prdmg/
grthweb/dddeisqu.htm

INDEX

INDEX

al-Haq, Mabub, 111
health 38–9, 77; services 25–6
Hinduism 52, 54
Hirsch, Fred, 95 100–1
Hungary 81

illiteracy 25–6
income: creation 44; distribution 66; per head 8–9, 11–13, 17–18, 30, 32, 46, 48, 50–2, 63, 65–6, 81, 92, 105, 114; world 18
India 25, 52, 54–5, 60–1, 80, 108; Kerala 25–6, 53
Indonesia 91, 108
Industrial Revolution 21, 37–8, 88, 101
industrialization 13, 17, 39, 49, 55, 93–4, 103, 114
industry 38, 97
inequality 7, 9, 18–19, 24, 28–34, 45, 66, 68, 76, 81–2, 85–6, 92, 98, 101, 103, 105–7, 110–11
inflation 59, 71, 78–9, 90, 106–9
International Monetary Fund (IMF) 90 1, 113
Iraq 27
Ireland, Republic of 17, 29–30
Islam 54
Italy 51, 86

Japan 12–14, 27, 48, 52, 57, 80, 112–13
Johnson, Lyndon, 77

Klingebeil, Daniela, 89–90
Korea 91

Landes, David, 14, 50–1
Latin America 17–18, 27–8, 46, 48, 51, 61, 87–8
Lebanon 27
Leeds 69–70
Leeson, Nick, 112

Maddison, Angus, 9
Malaysia 45, 111
malnutrition 8, 25–6
Malthus, Thomas, 35–37, 39, 41
Mao Tse-tung 14
market economy 9, 44, 55, 86, 99, 103
Marks, Howard, 69
Mexico 29, 88
Michie, Jonathan, 72
Middle East 17
Mishan, Ed, 95
Mongolia 84
mortality rate, infant 8, 38
Moss, Bernard, 72

Norway 27

OECD 57; Development Assistance Committee 110
output (per worker) 47–8

Patten, Chris, 57
Pergau Dam project 62
Philippines 51–2, 111
Poland 29
pollution 24, 95, 97–9
poor, the 7, 10, 15, 18–19, 30, 32–3, 36, 44–6, 55, 67, 81, 94–5, 99, 105, 107–8, 113 see also poverty
population 8–11, 13, 15, 18, 25, 35–43, 46; First World 11; growth 105
poverty 7–10, 12, 18–19, 20–30, 32–37, 39, 42–6, 48, 52–4, 56–7, 61, 65, 67, 69–72, 77–8, 80, 83, 85–8, 90, 92, 97, 99, 100, 103, 105–6, 110–11, 113; absolute 7–8, 17–21, 25, 28–30, 33, 35, 42, 46, 52, 65–6, 69, 80 2, 92, 104, 109; Eliminating World Poverty 10, 20, 35, 42, 44, 47, 55, 61–2; Human Poverty Index (UN) 25–6; income 25, 27–8, 110; line 21–2, 30, 46, 70; new 45, 48, 68, 76, 78–9, 83, 106–9 ; population 15, 59–60; relative 29–30, 65, 80–1; rural 17; urban 17, 37
privatization 82–4, 107
production 46, 105–6
productivity 31, 33, 36, 44–5, 47–48, 56
prosperity 9, 36–7, 65–6, 94
Protestantism 50–1, 53

quality of life 23, 30; see also capability

Reagan, Ronald, 32
redistribution 44
rich, the 7, 18–19, 30, 32, 67, 81, 99, 105, 111
Rowntree Foundation 29
Rowntree, Benjamin Seebohm, 21, 25
Russia 13–14, 81–4, 102, 106, 108

Sahara desert 17
Saudi Arabia 27
Second World 11, 22, 27–8, 40, 89, 93, 104
Sen, Amartya, 24, 52–4
service industries 73
Short, Clare, 57
Singapore 26, 45, 112
Singh, Manmohan, 54–5
Social Welfare 30–4, 76, 79–80, 90, 94, 114